Jehovah's Deception

By
Val Possidonio

Dedication

This book is dedicated to the countless individuals throughout history who, despite the weight of imposed dogma and the pervasive influence of carefully constructed narratives, dared to question, to seek, and to strive for a deeper understanding of the world around them. It is dedicated to those who, in the face of overwhelming societal pressures, maintained their intellectual curiosity and refused to accept convenient truths without critical examination. Their relentless pursuit of knowledge, their unwavering commitment to truth, even when uncomfortable or inconvenient, has paved the way for the investigation presented within these pages.

This work is also dedicated to the unsung heroes of historical inquiry, the meticulous researchers, the diligent scholars, and the often-overlooked archivists who have dedicated their lives to unearthing the fragments of our past, painstakingly piecing together the broken shards of history to reveal glimpses of forgotten realities. Their tireless efforts, often conducted in the face of adversity and skepticism, have made it possible to even begin to unravel the complex tapestry of human experience and expose the subtle machinations that have shaped our understanding of the divine. They have shown us that the past is not a monolithic entity, but a fluid landscape of interpretation, subject to revision and reevaluation.

Further, this dedication extends to those who have bravely challenged the status quo, the iconoclasts who have dared to question established power structures and expose the hidden agendas that often lie beneath the surface of social norms and religious practices. Their courage to challenge accepted narratives, even at personal risk, has demonstrated the importance of critical thinking and the necessity of challenging established orthodoxies. Their willingness to confront uncomfortable truths, however disturbing, serves as an inspiration for anyone seeking to understand the world beyond the confines of preconceived notions.

Finally, this book is dedicated to the future generations, to those who will inherit the legacy of past beliefs and the burden of past manipulations. It is my sincere hope that this work will serve as a catalyst for critical self-reflection, a prompt to analyze the underlying power structures that have shaped their understanding of reality. By understanding the past, we can arm ourselves against the insidious manipulations of the present and construct a future founded on truth, critical inquiry, and a commitment to intellectual freedom. May this work inspire a generation to seek truth, to question authority, and to build a world based on understanding rather than unquestioning acceptance. The path to liberation begins with understanding, and understanding begins with asking the difficult questions.

Table of Contents

Chapter 1 Unveiling the Deception 1

The Fabricated God Jehovah's Extraterrestrial Origins..........................1

The Seeds of Deception. Early Manipulation Tactics 5

The Usurpation of Power. The Fall of the Old Gods 8

The Construction of Religious Narrative Shaping Human Belief 13

The Long Shadow of Deception. Jehovah's Enduring Influence................17

Chapter 2 Deciphering Ancient Texts 22

Hidden Messages in Ancient Scriptures. Unveiling the Truth 22

Reinterpreting Mythology Symbols and Allegories of Deception 26

Archaeological Anomalies. Physical Evidence of the Extraterrestrial Presence 30

The Role of Secret Societies. Guardians of the Truth or Agents of Deception 34

Connecting the Dots. A Synthesis of Evidence...38

Chapter 3 The Psychological Impact of Belief 43

The Power of Belief. How Jehovah Manipulated Human Psychology........43

The Creation of Fear and Control. Maintaining the Status Quo 49

The Role of Ritual and Ceremony Reinforcing Belief and Control 54

The Suppression of Dissent. Maintaining the Illusion of Authority 59

Breaking Free from the Chains of Belief. A Path to Enlightenment 64

Chapter 4 The Alien Agenda..69

Jehovah's Ultimate Goals. What Does He Really Want..............................69

The Manipulation of Resources. Jehovah's Control over Earth's Wealth...74

The Control of Humanity. A Long-Term Strategy for Domination............79

The Threat of Intervention. Extraterrestrial Conflicts and Humanity's Role 84

The Potential for Resistance. Challenging Jehovah's Authority 89

Chapter 5: A New Dawn 94

Reinterpreting History. A Revised Timeline of Human Events 94
Rediscovering Our True Heritage. Reclaiming Our Spiritual Identity 99
The Future of Spirituality Beyond the Control of Jehovah 104
Embracing Critical Thinking. The Path to a More Authentic Existence .. 108
A Call to Action. Taking Responsibility for Our Future 113
Acknowledgments 118
Glossary 119
Author Biography 120

Chapter 1
Unveiling the Deception

The Fabricated God Jehovah's Extraterrestrial Origins

The accepted narrative paints Jehovah as the omnipotent creator, the benevolent shepherd guiding humanity through millennia. But what if this carefully constructed image masks a far more sinister reality? What if the God worshipped by billions is not the divine being he claims to be, but a powerful extraterrestrial entity, an Annunaki, who meticulously crafted a deceptive religious system to achieve his own ends? This is the radical proposition that lies at the heart of our investigation.

Our journey begins by peering into the distant past, to a time when Earth was a young planet, teeming with nascent life, and visited by beings far more advanced than humanity. The Annunaki, a race possessing technological capabilities beyond our current comprehension, are described in ancient Sumerian texts as possessing god-like powers, capable of manipulating the very fabric of existence. These accounts, often dismissed as myth or legend, suddenly take on a new significance when considered through the lens of a deliberate, extraterrestrial intervention in human history.

One such account, the Epic of Gilgamesh, narrates the exploits of a demigod king, possessing superhuman strength and wisdom. This figure, often interpreted as a mythical hero, could be interpreted as a representative, perhaps even a veiled reference, to one of the Annunaki who initially came to Earth. These beings, according to these ancient accounts, engaged in various projects on Earth, some benevolent, some driven by self-interest. It is within this complex tapestry of early interactions that Jehovah's story begins.

Archaeological evidence, often overlooked or dismissed by mainstream scholars, could lend credence to this extraordinary theory. Sites like Gobekli Tepe, a pre-pottery Neolithic site in

Turkey dating back to 10,000 BCE, reveal sophisticated architectural and astronomical knowledge far beyond the capabilities of the purportedly primitive societies of that era. Could such advanced structures have been built with the assistance, or even under the direction, of a technologically advanced extraterrestrial civilization? The possibility cannot be dismissed outright.

Jehovah's role within this advanced civilization is initially unclear. The ancient texts offer tantalizing glimpses of a complex power dynamic, with different Annunaki factions vying for dominance, not unlike the rivalries and power struggles observed throughout human history. While some Annunaki focused on advancing human civilization, others pursued more self-serving goals. Jehovah, according to our interpretation of these texts, belonged to the latter group. He wasn't a mere participant; he possessed an inherent ambition, a hunger for power that far outstripped his initial role in the ancient Earth project.

The specifics of Jehovah's origins within the Annunaki civilization remain shrouded in mystery. It's possible he was a member of a lesser clan, a relatively insignificant figure who ascended to power through cunning and manipulation. Or, perhaps, he originated from a more prominent lineage, only to be driven by a personal ambition so profound that he betrayed his own kind. The ancient texts do not offer clear answers, but they do provide enough clues to suggest a complex and potentially violent struggle for supremacy within the Annunaki ranks.

The Book of Enoch, a pseudepigraphical text considered canonical by some religious sects, offers further support for this hypothesis. The text speaks of the Nephilim, offspring of the "watchers" (often interpreted as fallen angels), who wreaked havoc upon the Earth. This could be a coded description of the Annunaki, their interactions with humanity resulting in offspring that possessed a mixture of human and extraterrestrial characteristics. This narrative fits seamlessly into our hypothesis, illustrating a conflict between different factions within the Annunaki civilization.

Jehovah's initial approach was characterized by subtle manipulation and deceptive tactics. He didn't openly seize power; rather, he weaved his way into existing power structures, exploiting pre-existing religious beliefs and societal hierarchies. He subtly influenced the development of early religious practices, gradually shaping human perception and belief to align with his ambitions. His tactics were those of a seasoned manipulator, patiently weaving a complex web of deception, slowly but surely building his influence.

The comparison with the historical concept of the "divine right of kings" is highly pertinent here. The belief in a divinely ordained ruler, a king whose authority stems directly from God, is a powerful tool for maintaining control. Jehovah, in this interpretation, masterfully appropriated this concept, positioning himself as the ultimate source of authority, the supreme being to whom all others must submit. This carefully crafted narrative provided him with the legitimacy he required to consolidate his power and maintain his control over humanity.

The fall of the old gods, as described in some ancient texts, is not a metaphorical event but a literal power struggle. Jehovah, through his manipulation and cunning, ultimately triumphed, seizing control from other Annunaki entities. The subsequent religious system he established was designed not to guide humanity towards spiritual enlightenment but to serve his own ends. This system, meticulously crafted over centuries, provided him with the tools necessary to control human behavior, resources, and ultimately, the planet itself.

The construction of the religious narrative is a crucial component of Jehovah's strategy. Creation myths, carefully worded stories, and intricate rituals, all served to reinforce his authority and shape human perceptions. Sacred texts were manipulated, historical events were distorted, and a complex theological structure was erected, effectively shielding the truth about his origins and intentions. The resulting religious dogma served as a powerful tool of control, shaping human thought and behavior for millennia.

The lasting influence of Jehovah's deception is undeniable. The religions that arose from his machinations continue to shape the world, influencing our values, our laws, our wars, and our very understanding of ourselves. The long shadow of his manipulation stretches across history, revealing a disturbing pattern of control and manipulation masked behind a veil of piety and religious fervor. This is not a tale of benevolent guidance, but a narrative of calculated deception and carefully cultivated power. Understanding this reality is the first step towards breaking free from the constraints of a manufactured belief system and embracing a more authentic understanding of our place in the universe. The path forward requires critical thinking, a willingness to question established dogma, and a commitment to uncovering the hidden truths of our past. Only then can we begin to build a future free from the enduring legacy of the fabricated God.

The Seeds of Deception. Early Manipulation Tactics

Jehovah's ascent to power was not a sudden coup, but a meticulously orchestrated campaign of subtle manipulation spanning centuries. He understood the power of gradual influence, a slow erosion of existing belief systems, paving the way for his own self-proclaimed divinity. His strategy wasn't brute force, but the art of the long con, preying on human vulnerabilities and exploiting pre-existing societal structures.

The early interactions between the Annunaki and nascent human civilizations provided fertile ground for his machinations. Ancient societies, awestruck by the seemingly godlike powers of these extraterrestrials, readily attributed divine origins to their advanced technology and seemingly miraculous feats. Jehovah recognized this inherent predisposition towards awe and wonder, deftly capitalizing on it to elevate his status. He didn't introduce an entirely new religion; rather, he subtly infiltrated and reshaped existing belief systems, gradually weaving his narrative into the fabric of already established faiths.

Consider the prevalence of sun worship in many ancient cultures. The sun, a life-giving force, was naturally venerated as a powerful deity. Jehovah, adept at symbolism and ritual, cleverly associated himself with the sun's power, gradually shifting the focus from the celestial body itself to his own person. He strategically placed himself as the intermediary between humanity and the sun's life-giving energy, a position that cemented his growing influence. This subtle shift from sun worship to a more personalized deity, Jehovah as the embodiment of solar power, was a masterstroke of manipulative genius.

Similarly, the concept of kingship played a crucial role in Jehovah's ascent. Early civilizations often attributed divine right to their rulers, believing their authority stemmed directly from the gods. Jehovah cleverly exploited this belief, positioning himself as the ultimate source of royal power. He subtly influenced the narratives surrounding kingship, ensuring that his image was inextricably linked with the legitimacy of earthly rulers. By associating himself with power structures, he not only gained influence but also legitimized his own claim to divine status. This strategic alignment with existing power dynamics ensured the smooth transition of his fabricated divinity into the mainstream.

His manipulation extended beyond established institutions; it seeped into the very fabric of human storytelling and mythology. Ancient myths and epics, often passed down through oral traditions, provided a malleable medium for Jehovah to subtly reshape human perception. He didn't simply erase existing narratives; instead, he carefully altered and reinterpreted them, weaving his own persona into the very heart of these foundational stories. By controlling the narrative, he controlled the collective consciousness of humanity, slowly eroding any potential opposition to his growing power.

A significant element of his strategy involved the manipulation of prophets and oracles. These individuals, often revered for their supposed connection to the divine, were susceptible to Jehovah's subtle influence. Through dreams, visions, and even direct communication, he would impart his messages, ensuring their dissemination among the populace. This tactic was particularly effective, as prophetic pronouncements carried immense weight within society, reinforcing Jehovah's image as the all-powerful deity. These prophecies, subtly crafted to reinforce his dominance and legitimize his actions, created a potent tool of social control.

Furthermore, Jehovah's control extended to the development of early religious rituals and practices. The careful crafting of ceremonies, sacrifices, and prayers served not only to instill piety but also to reinforce his authority. These rituals, meticulously designed, created a powerful cycle of dependency, cementing the faithful's submission to his power. The regularity and repetition of these actions, coupled with the emotional weight associated with religious observance, served to further ingrain his dominance within the collective consciousness.

The manipulation of sacred texts, once these were codified, became another crucial aspect of Jehovah's strategy. The carefully chosen words, the deliberate omissions, and the strategic insertion of passages all served to reinforce his narrative and suppress any alternative perspectives. Over time, these texts became the foundation of organized religion, perpetuating the deception and solidifying Jehovah's control over generations to come. The power of the written word, once in his hands, became a formidable weapon in his ongoing campaign of manipulation.

The construction of temples and sacred sites also played a key role in establishing his dominion. These structures, often monumental in scale and architectural sophistication, served as powerful symbols of Jehovah's power and authority. Their design, their placement, and their very existence reinforced his control, physically manifesting his dominance across the landscape. These sites weren't merely places of worship; they were carefully constructed monuments intended to impress and intimidate, serving as constant reminders of Jehovah's power.

The long-term consequences of Jehovah's early manipulations are still felt today. The religious structures he established, the beliefs he cultivated, and the control mechanisms he put in place continue to shape human societies, influencing everything from political structures to personal ethics. Understanding the origins of these systems, the subtle deception at their core, is the first step in breaking free from their pervasive influence. The path forward involves a critical examination of the historical narrative, a willingness to question long-held assumptions, and a commitment to uncovering the hidden truths about our past. Only through such critical engagement can we hope to liberate ourselves from the manipulative legacy of a fabricated god. The dismantling of this fabricated reality requires a thorough understanding of its roots, its methods, and its enduring impact upon humanity. The seeds of deception, sown millennia ago, continue to bear poisonous fruit, and only by unearthing those seeds can we hope to cultivate a more authentic and equitable future.

The Usurpation of Power. The Fall of the Old Gods

The narrative surrounding Jehovah's ascension is not a singular event, but a complex tapestry woven from threads of deceit, manipulation, and strategic alliances. While he presented himself as a benevolent creator, the evidence suggests a ruthless campaign to consolidate power, culminating in the subjugation of other Annunaki and the establishment of a religiously enforced global hegemony. Ancient texts, often fragmented and shrouded in allegory, whisper of a rebellion, a struggle for supremacy among these celestial beings, a cosmic war fought not with weapons of fire, but with the subtle tools of influence and the manipulation of human belief.

Several Sumerian cuneiform tablets, painstakingly deciphered and interpreted, hint at the existence of a council of Annunaki, a governing body tasked with overseeing the Earth project. These tablets, often disregarded by mainstream scholarship, suggest a period of relative harmony and cooperation between the different Annunaki factions, each with their own areas of expertise and influence. This period of collaborative governance, however, was destined to be short-lived. The tablets depict Jehovah not as a leading member of this council, but as a cunning strategist, slowly gaining influence through his mastery of human psychology and his ability to exploit existing societal structures.

The subtle shift in power dynamics is evident in the changing iconography associated with these celestial beings. Early representations of the Annunaki depict them as relatively similar in stature and power, a visual representation of the council's collective authority. However, as Jehovah's influence grew, his depiction morphed. The imagery shifted from a figure of relative equality to one of towering dominance, reflecting his usurpation of authority and the consolidation of power. This change in iconography mirrors the shift in societal power structures, a testament to Jehovah's successful manipulation of human perception.

The downfall of other Annunaki, alluded to in fragmented narratives and obscure passages within ancient texts, is not a straightforward event, but a series of calculated moves on

Jehovah's part. He didn't necessarily eliminate his rivals through force, but rather through a combination of subtle manipulation, strategic alliances, and the dissemination of carefully crafted narratives designed to discredit and delegitimize his opponents. These narratives, passed down through generations in both oral and written forms, portray Jehovah's rivals as malevolent, destructive entities, thus justifying his actions and reinforcing his position as the sole legitimate authority.

The manipulation of religious narratives played a critical role in consolidating Jehovah's power. He subtly altered or suppressed stories that contradicted his own self-serving narrative, weaving a story of divine election and predetermined destiny. The concept of a chosen people, often associated with specific ethnic groups, served to strengthen his hold over these populations, creating a system of religious loyalty and obedience. This carefully constructed narrative of chosenness not only cemented his authority but also sowed the seeds of inter-group conflict, diverting attention away from his own actions and solidifying his control.

One compelling example lies in the varying interpretations of the flood myth. While many cultures relate the flood to a divine punishment for humanity's wickedness, Jehovah's version presents a significantly different interpretation. In his narrative, the flood serves as a tool of purification, a divine cleansing that paves the way for a new order, with himself as the chosen leader of this new era. This self-serving interpretation not only elevates his status but also justifies the elimination of his rivals, presenting their destruction as a necessary precursor to a divinely ordained future. This strategic rewriting of history, repeated across various cultures, solidified his image as the sole legitimate divine authority.

Furthermore, the establishment of a centralized religious system solidified Jehovah's control. The construction of grand temples and the establishment of standardized rituals created a potent system of social control, reinforcing his authority and ensuring the propagation of his fabricated narratives. These religious structures became not merely places of worship, but powerful symbols of his dominion, reinforcing his power through architecture, ritual, and social structure. The standardized religious practices created a powerful sense of community and shared identity, further enhancing Jehovah's control and influence.

The creation of a priestly class, loyal to Jehovah and trained in the intricacies of his religious system, proved to be another critical element in his scheme. These priests acted as intermediaries between Jehovah and the populace, disseminating his messages and enforcing his authority. This hierarchical system served to concentrate power within a select group, ensuring the perpetuation of his authority and the suppression of any potential challenges to his reign. The power dynamics created through this system ensured the continued propagation of Jehovah's narrative, even long after his initial interventions.

The long-term consequences of Jehovah's actions are far-reaching and deeply impactful. His carefully crafted religious system, built upon a foundation of deception, continues to shape human societies, influencing our values, our behaviors, and our understanding of the world. The remnants of his manipulative strategies are still evident in modern religious institutions, social structures, and political systems. To understand the present, we must first confront the manipulations of the past. By peeling back the layers of deception, by meticulously examining the ancient texts and reinterpreting the narratives, we can begin to understand the true extent of Jehovah's influence and the lasting impact of his usurpation of power.

The seemingly seamless transition from a pluralistic belief system to a monotheistic one was not an organic evolution, but the carefully orchestrated result of a celestial power struggle. This struggle, largely hidden from plain sight, played out on the stage of human history, with far-reaching consequences that extend to the present day. By critically analyzing ancient texts, deciphering the subtle manipulations inherent within religious narratives, and understanding the power dynamics at play, we begin to unravel the intricate web of deception that has shrouded humanity for millennia. The story of Jehovah's rise to power is a chilling tale of manipulation, a stark reminder of the fragility of truth and the enduring power of belief.

The subsequent suppression of alternative narratives accounts that challenged Jehovah's supremacy or revealed the truth about the Annunaki was equally crucial to his lasting influence. The destruction or alteration of competing mythologies, the selective preservation of "convenient" narratives, and the systematic elimination of dissenting voices all contributed to the consolidation of Jehovah's dominance. This was not merely the suppression of information; it was a rewriting of history itself, a carefully crafted narrative designed to cement Jehovah's power and ensure the continued acceptance of his self-proclaimed divinity. The control of narrative became a crucial weapon in his arsenal, shaping not just religious belief but also the very fabric of human society.

Further research into forgotten languages, long-lost dialects, and marginalized cultural traditions reveals fragments of alternative narratives, whispers of a different past. These fragments, pieced together with painstaking care, reveal glimpses of a time before Jehovah's dominance, a time of greater diversity and a more complex understanding of the divine. These alternative perspectives, often ignored or dismissed by mainstream scholarship, offer critical insights into Jehovah's manipulation, providing a counter-narrative to the officially sanctioned version of events. The recovery and interpretation of these marginalized perspectives is not simply an academic exercise; it is a crucial step in the process of reclaiming our history and understanding the full extent of Jehovah's deceptive actions.

The implications of this revelation are profound and far-reaching. It challenges not only our understanding of religious history, but also our understanding of ourselves and our place in the universe. It suggests that the very foundations of many of our beliefs and institutions are rooted in deception, raising questions about the nature of truth, the power of manipulation, and the responsibility we have to critically examine the narratives that shape our lives. The journey towards a more authentic understanding of our past, and a more truthful future, requires a willingness to confront uncomfortable truths and to challenge the established narratives that have shaped our perception of reality. The unveiling of Jehovah's deception is not merely a historical account; it is a call to critical self-reflection and a challenge to the very foundations of our understanding of reality. The task that lies ahead is not merely one of intellectual inquiry, but a profound spiritual and existential reckoning.

The Construction of Religious Narrative Shaping Human Belief

The meticulous construction of Jehovah's religious narrative was a masterpiece of social engineering, a carefully crafted system designed to control human behavior and secure his enduring power. It wasn't simply a matter of proclaiming divine authority; it was a strategic campaign, executed over centuries, involving the manipulation of myths, rituals, and doctrines to shape human beliefs and maintain a rigid social hierarchy. This section delves into the methods employed, revealing the intricate mechanisms used to solidify Jehovah's reign and suppress dissenting voices.

Central to this construction was the creation myth itself. The narrative of creation, as presented by Jehovah's followers, carefully omitted any mention of the Annunaki council, the pre-existing collaborative governance, and the power struggles that led to Jehovah's ascension. Instead, it presented a simplified, self-serving account, emphasizing Jehovah's sole role in creation and his absolute authority over the universe. This streamlined narrative, disseminated through generations via oral tradition and carefully curated written texts, minimized any complexities that might challenge his unique status. The absence of alternative creation accounts, accounts which might have portrayed a more collaborative or chaotic genesis, was crucial in establishing the singularity of Jehovah's power. The story was meticulously designed to reinforce the idea of a single, omnipotent creator, thus eliminating any possibility of competing deities or divine authorities.

The manipulation extended beyond the creation myth. The flood narrative, as previously discussed, serves as a prime example. While other cultures may have depicted the flood as a catastrophic natural event or a punishment for collective human failings, Jehovah's version positioned the flood as a divinely orchestrated purification, a cleansing necessary to pave the way for a new, divinely ordained era under his leadership. This reframing of a cataclysmic event served not only to elevate his status but also to erase the memory of the prior era and its potential challenges to his power. It was a strategic act of historical revisionism, rewriting the past to serve the present.

Furthermore, the carefully constructed rituals and ceremonies served as powerful instruments of social control. These meticulously designed practices, often imbued with symbolic meaning and steeped in ancient traditions, reinforced Jehovah's authority and instilled a sense of awe and reverence in his followers. The standardized nature of these rituals, from the specific words used in prayers to the precise movements performed during ceremonies, further cemented Jehovah's control. Deviation from these prescribed practices was often met with severe consequences, fostering obedience and ensuring the perpetuation of the religious system. The architecture itself played a critical role. The construction of magnificent temples, often situated at strategic locations and designed to impress, served as powerful symbols of Jehovah's dominance. These structures weren't merely places of worship; they were tangible manifestations of his power, reinforcing his authority through sheer scale and architectural grandeur.

The development of a codified system of laws and doctrines further solidified Jehovah's control. These meticulously crafted laws, presented as divinely ordained, regulated every aspect of life, from personal conduct to social interactions. This comprehensive legal system, seamlessly integrated with the religious framework, ensured the strict enforcement of Jehovah's will and minimized the possibility of dissent. The penalties for violating these laws often carried severe religious and societal consequences, solidifying obedience and maintaining the existing power structures.

The manipulation of sacred texts also played a critical role. The texts were not simply preserved; they were carefully selected, edited, and interpreted to support Jehovah's narrative. Passages that contradicted his authority were either removed or reinterpreted to align with the dominant ideology, creating a self-consistent, though fundamentally flawed, account of the past. The process of canonization, the selection of texts deemed authoritative, was a crucial step in establishing a monolithic religious doctrine, one that left little room for alternative interpretations or competing narratives. The deliberate suppression of alternative texts, representing different perspectives or challenging narratives, ensured the dominance of Jehovah's carefully constructed worldview.

The creation of a priestly class served as another critical mechanism in perpetuating Jehovah's control. This highly trained and organized group acted as intermediaries between Jehovah and his followers, interpreting scripture, performing rituals, and disseminating religious doctrine. By controlling the interpretation of sacred texts and the administration of religious practices, the priestly class ensured the continued propagation of Jehovah's narrative and suppressed any potential challenges to his authority. The hierarchical structure of the priesthood, with its distinct levels of authority and responsibility, reinforced the existing power dynamics and cemented Jehovah's position at the apex of the religious system.

The long-term consequences of Jehovah's meticulous construction of the religious narrative are profound and far-reaching. The narratives he crafted continue to shape societies, influencing our values, our behaviors, and our understanding of the world. The influence of his manipulated myths and distorted historical accounts can still be seen in modern religious institutions, political systems, and social structures. Examining these enduring legacies allows for a deeper understanding of the subtle, yet powerful, ways in which religious narratives can shape human behavior and maintain power structures. The meticulously crafted religious system, built upon a foundation of deception, continues to exert its influence, underscoring the importance of critical examination and the ongoing need for a more truthful understanding of our past. Unveiling the deception is crucial not just for historical accuracy, but also for a more authentic spiritual journey and a clearer understanding of our present reality. The project of deciphering and reinterpreting these historical narratives remains a task that demands continued vigilance and critical analysis. The weight of this legacy rests upon our collective ability to critically examine and challenge the established narratives that have long shaped our understanding of the world, ourselves, and our relationship with the divine. Only through diligent scrutiny can we hope to unravel the intricacies of this historical deception and forge a path towards a more truthful and equitable future.

The Long Shadow of Deception. Jehovah's Enduring Influence

The insidious nature of Jehovah's deception extends far beyond the initial manipulation of myths and rituals. Its tendrils have woven themselves deeply into the fabric of human history, shaping civilizations and influencing the very course of human events. The consequences, felt across millennia, are a testament to the enduring power of skillfully crafted narratives and the fragility of truth when confronted by carefully constructed falsehoods.

One of the most significant long-term consequences is the establishment of rigid social hierarchies that mirrored the celestial hierarchy presented by Jehovah's narrative. The divinely ordained authority, supposedly granted to Jehovah, was reflected in the earthly power structures that emerged, where kings and emperors claimed divine right to rule, justifying their authority through a lineage supposedly tracing back to the chosen people or favored individuals. This legitimization of earthly power structures through divine sanction had profound implications, often resulting in the oppression of the masses and the consolidation of wealth and power in the hands of a privileged few. The inherent inequality woven into Jehovah's narrative provided a theological justification for existing social injustices, making these inequalities appear divinely ordained rather than socially constructed.

This divinely sanctioned hierarchy impacted not only the political landscape but also the economic and social fabric of societies. The control over resources, land, and labor often fell into the hands of those claiming a privileged position within the established religious order. The priestly class, acting as intermediaries between Jehovah and the populace, benefited significantly from this system, accumulating wealth and influence while reinforcing their own privileged status. The economic disparities created and sustained by this hierarchical system have left a long shadow, perpetuating inequalities that continue to plague societies to this day. The idea of a "chosen people" further reinforced these divisions, creating an inherent us-versus-them mentality that has fueled conflict and prejudice for centuries.

The impact on the development of ethical systems also deserves consideration. While Jehovah's followers promoted certain ethical codes, these were often intertwined with the maintenance of power and the reinforcement of social hierarchies. The emphasis on obedience, adherence to strict rules, and punishment for transgression created a moral framework that sometimes prioritized conformity over critical thinking or individual conscience. The fear of divine retribution, skillfully cultivated through generations of religious indoctrination, fostered a climate of compliance that stifled dissent and individual expression. This emphasis on obedience often came at the expense of compassion, empathy, and a nuanced understanding of ethical dilemmas. The concept of divine justice, often interpreted as retributive and harsh, contributed to cycles of violence and intolerance.

The long shadow of Jehovah's influence also extends to subsequent religious movements. Many religions that emerged after Jehovah's dominance incorporated aspects of his narrative, either consciously or unconsciously. The concept of a single, all-powerful God, the emphasis on a linear history culminating in a messianic figure, and the importance of a divinely revealed scripture, all echoes of Jehovah's religious construction, became widespread themes, influencing the development of numerous belief systems. This adoption and adaptation of Jehovah's narrative illustrate the pervasive influence of his meticulously constructed system, demonstrating its enduring capacity to shape religious thought and practice. The very structure of many religious organizations, with their hierarchical power structures and emphasis on dogma, reflects the organizational model established under Jehovah's reign.

The persistence of Jehovah's influence can also be seen in modern political systems. The concept of the divine right of kings, although largely discredited, continues to resonate in certain political ideologies and worldviews. The use of religious rhetoric to justify political power, to legitimize violence, and to rally support for specific causes, remains a potent tool. The manipulation of religious narratives to promote political agendas, to justify wars, or to suppress dissent continues to be a concern. This persistent influence underscores the importance of critically examining the relationship between religion and politics and the ways in which religious belief can be exploited for political gain.

The consequences of Jehovah's actions extend to the very way we understand history. The deliberate suppression of alternative narratives and the manipulation of historical accounts created a skewed understanding of the past, which continues to shape our interpretation of events and our sense of identity. This distortion of historical narratives has implications not only for historical scholarship but also for our understanding of ourselves and our place in the world. The ongoing effort to recover and reinterpret suppressed or distorted historical accounts is crucial for a more comprehensive and accurate understanding of the past.

Moreover, the ongoing effects of Jehovah's deception are evident in the psychological and emotional impact on individuals and societies. The manipulation of belief systems can lead to a sense of helplessness, a diminished sense of agency, and a reliance on external authority rather than critical thinking and independent judgment. The fear of divine punishment and the pressure to conform to rigid religious doctrines can stifle personal growth, creativity, and intellectual exploration. The enduring legacy of Jehovah's religious construction raises significant questions about the relationship between belief, power, and control. Understanding the historical context of these beliefs is crucial in analyzing their present-day impact and working towards a more balanced and informed approach to faith and spirituality.

The examination of Jehovah's enduring influence allows for a deeper understanding of the intricate interplay between religion, power, and the human psyche. His carefully constructed religious system, built upon a foundation of deception, serves as a case study in the potent capacity of narratives to shape human behavior and control societies. The long-term consequences of these manipulations are profound and far-reaching, continuing to influence our values, our beliefs, and our understanding of the world. The legacy of Jehovah's deception underscores the critical importance of critical thinking, historical awareness, and a commitment to truth-seeking in our pursuit of a more authentic and meaningful existence. This requires a continuous effort to challenge established narratives, to question authority, and to strive for a more just and equitable future, free from the insidious influence of carefully constructed falsehoods. The journey towards a more truthful and liberated understanding of our past and present is a continuous process that demands ongoing vigilance and a commitment to challenging the power structures that perpetuate deception. Only then can we hope to overcome the long shadow cast by Jehovah's manipulation and build a future founded on truth, justice, and genuine spiritual growth.

REFLECTION: The one who is named cannot be the Creator. The one named is not God but rather an entity, an energy or force. The true God and Creator does not have a pronounceable name or a name that is manifested in any way. This is the truth of galactic energy and also of the Kabbalah.

Chapter 2
Deciphering Ancient Texts

Hidden Messages in Ancient Scriptures. Unveiling the Truth

The insidious manipulation woven into Jehovah's narrative extends beyond the broad strokes of historical influence and societal structures. It delves into the very fabric of the texts themselves, the sacred scriptures that form the bedrock of countless faiths. The scriptures, often presented as divinely inspired and immutable, are in fact subject to interpretation, and it is through this very act of interpretation that Jehovah's deception has been most effectively perpetuated. By controlling the narrative, by shaping the accepted understanding of these texts, the architects of Jehovah's power maintained their grip on the hearts and minds of generations. But closer scrutiny reveals cracks in this carefully constructed edifice, revealing hidden messages and alternative readings that challenge the established orthodoxy.

Consider, for example, the Book of Genesis. The traditional interpretation, meticulously cultivated over centuries, presents a linear narrative of creation, fall, and redemption, a narrative that perfectly supports Jehovah's hierarchical structure and the concept of divinely ordained authority. Adam and Eve's transgression, interpreted as an act of defiance against divine authority, becomes the justification for human suffering and the need for a divinely ordained savior. However, a closer reading, devoid of the centuries of imposed theological overlay, reveals a far more nuanced and potentially subversive text. The serpent, often portrayed as a villainous tempter, can also be seen as a symbol of knowledge and self-awareness, questioning the inherent authority of Jehovah's pronouncements. The act of eating the forbidden fruit, instead of being a display of sinful disobedience, could be understood as a courageous step towards self-discovery and the pursuit of understanding, a crucial element often suppressed in traditional interpretations.

Similarly, the flood narrative, a tale of divine punishment and the chosen few, can be reexamined. The chosen people, Noah and his family, are saved not because of inherent piety, but rather through their subservience to Jehovah's commands. The destruction of the world is often interpreted as a divine act of judgment, but an alternative reading might view it as a metaphor for societal upheaval or an ecological catastrophe. By focusing on the narrative of survival and rebuilding, rather than the destructive power of Jehovah, we can discover a more complex and less theologically driven interpretation. The details of the ark's construction and the specific animals chosen become less significant than the overarching theme of perseverance and the creation of a new beginning. The emphasis shifts from divine punishment to the resilience of life.

Moving beyond Genesis, the Psalms offer another fertile ground for reinterpretation. The seemingly unquestioning praise of Jehovah contained within many psalms could be argued to be expressions of fear and desperation rather than sincere devotion. Many psalms detail suffering, lament, and appeals for mercy, suggesting a far less harmonious relationship between humanity and their creator than the traditional readings suggest. These passages, often overlooked in favor of the more celebratory hymns, hint at a more complex and potentially troubling relationship with the divine. They offer a glimpse into a world where faith is not necessarily unwavering, and where supplication is not always met with benevolent grace. The emotional depth and raw honesty expressed in these psalms suggest a more nuanced understanding of human spirituality, one that cannot be fully captured by a simplistic reading that only highlights passages of praise and adoration.

The prophetic books of the Old Testament, often used to justify wars and conquests, also reveal a less clear-cut picture when examined without the imposed lens of centuries of theological interpretation. The pronouncements of doom and destruction often attributed to the divine will might be reinterpreted as critiques of societal injustices and warnings against unchecked power. The prophets themselves, frequently portrayed as unwavering messengers of Jehovah, can be seen as critical voices, challenging the status quo and calling for social reform. Their pronouncements, while often framed within a religious context, address issues of social equity, economic oppression, and political corruption, themes that resonate even today. By focusing on the social and political critiques contained within these texts, we gain a deeper understanding of the historical context in which they were written, and we can separate the prophetic messages from the later theological interpretations that twisted their meaning to suit specific power structures.

The New Testament also offers grounds for re-interpretation. The Gospels, while presented as accounts of a divinely ordained savior, can be read through the lens of social history. Jesus's teachings, often interpreted as purely spiritual, also address social and economic issues. His actions, such as the cleansing of the Temple, can be understood as acts of political defiance, challenging the corruption of the religious establishment and advocating for social justice. The parables, often seen as allegorical tales with purely spiritual meanings, can be analyzed from a socio-economic perspective, revealing insightful commentaries on the complexities of human relationships and power dynamics within society. His interaction with the marginalized members of society, the sick, the poor, and the outcast, can be seen as an act of social inclusion and a challenge to the established social order. By focusing on the social context of Jesus' ministry, we move beyond simplistic spiritual readings, uncovering a deeper message of social justice.

The exploration of these texts requires a shift in perspective. We must move beyond the traditional, often dogma-laden interpretations and engage in critical analysis, drawing on tools from history, sociology, and literary criticism. This means acknowledging the biases inherent in the transmission and interpretation of these texts over centuries, acknowledging that power structures have actively shaped how these texts have been understood. We need to look at the texts not just as divinely inspired pronouncements, but as cultural artifacts, products of their specific historical and social contexts. This approach requires careful attention to linguistic nuances, literary devices, and the historical circumstances in which these texts were written, read, and interpreted.

The identification of hidden messages is not about rejecting faith altogether. Instead, it is about reclaiming the power of critical thinking and fostering a more nuanced understanding of these ancient texts. It is about acknowledging the complexity of human spirituality and the ways in which religious narratives have been manipulated to serve the interests of power. By peeling back layers of theological interpretation and historical distortion, we can uncover alternative meanings and interpretations, challenging the dominant narratives and revealing the truth behind Jehovah's deception. This is not a quest for a single, definitive truth, but rather a journey towards a deeper and more nuanced understanding of these ancient texts and their enduring impact on human history and spirituality. The journey involves engaging with multiple perspectives, respecting the diversity of interpretations, and recognizing that the understanding of sacred texts is a continuous and evolving process. The goal is not to discard the texts themselves but to reclaim them from the manipulative grip of those who have used them to consolidate power and perpetuate injustice. This process requires a commitment to open inquiry, a willingness to question established authorities, and an unwavering dedication to the pursuit of truth. The uncovering of these hidden messages is a critical step towards a more authentic and liberated spiritual experience.

Reinterpreting Mythology Symbols and Allegories of Deception

The deceptive nature of Jehovah's narrative extends beyond the textual manipulation of scripture; it permeates the very foundation of mythology and symbolism, subtly altering cultural narratives to reinforce its authority. Ancient myths, often presented as simple tales of gods and heroes, become coded messages when examined through a critical lens. These seemingly innocent stories were instruments of power, cleverly designed to conceal the true nature of Jehovah and its machinations.

Consider the ubiquitous symbol of the serpent. In many ancient cultures, the serpent was a powerful symbol of fertility, healing, and wisdom, a creature embodying both creation and destruction. However, in the Jehovah narrative, the serpent is demonized, cast as the embodiment of evil, the deceiver who led humanity astray. This demonization, a deliberate act of symbolic manipulation, effectively neutralized a potent symbol that could potentially challenge Jehovah's authority. By associating the serpent with temptation and sin, Jehovah simultaneously undermined its positive connotations and asserted its own superior position as the sole source of morality and order. This subtle shift in meaning, achieved through careful narrative control, reveals the extent of Jehovah's manipulative tactics. The power of the serpent's original symbolism, one that resonated with ancient cultures across the globe, was systematically suppressed, replaced with a negatively-charged image designed to maintain a hierarchical structure.

The story of the Great Flood presents another case study. While often interpreted as a divine punishment for humanity's wickedness, a closer analysis reveals a potentially different narrative. The flood, in many ancient myths, represents a cyclical renewal, a cleansing process that precedes a new beginning. The destruction and subsequent rebuilding could be seen as a metaphor for the cyclical nature of life, death, and rebirth, a powerful symbol that predates the Jehovah's narrative. However, by framing the flood as a punishment from a vengeful deity, Jehovah subtly shifts the focus from a natural cycle of renewal to an act of divine retribution, solidifying its role as the supreme judge and arbiter of human destiny. The selection of Noah, not for his exceptional virtue but for his obedience, further reinforces this message of subservience to divine authority. The story thereby transforms from a celebration of cyclical renewal into a testament to Jehovah's power and humanity's utter dependence on its capricious will.

The mythological figures themselves often serve as vessels for coded messages. Consider the numerous creation myths that exist across cultures. Many involve a primordial chaos, a state of formlessness and potential, from which order emerges. This chaos, often portrayed as a threatening force, represents the unknown, the untamed aspects of existence that challenge the rigid structures imposed by Jehovah. In the Jehovah's creation myth, chaos is subdued, transformed into a neatly organized cosmos, mirroring the suppression of any potential threat to its authority. This act of narrative control, the taming of chaos and the imposition of order, becomes a reflection of Jehovah's own method of maintaining power.

Furthermore, many ancient goddesses, representing fertility, nurturing, and life-giving power, were effectively marginalized or demonized in the Jehovah's narrative. These figures, often associated with earth-based spiritualties, offered alternative pathways to understanding the world and human existence, pathways that challenged the patriarchal structure imposed by the Jehovah's narrative. Their suppression reflects a deliberate attempt to consolidate power by controlling access to spiritual experiences and limiting the diversity of religious expression. The replacement of these powerful female figures with a more austere and less nurturing divine presence is yet another manifestation of the subtle manipulation inherent in Jehovah's narrative.

The use of allegory in ancient myths provides another layer of deception. Animal symbolism, a pervasive element in many cultures, is consistently reinterpreted within the Jehovah's narrative to reinforce the message of obedience and fear. The lion, representing strength and courage, might be used to symbolize the power of Jehovah, reinforcing the image of a powerful and unchallengeable deity. Conversely, animals associated with trickery or rebellion, like the fox or the raven, are often demonized, further solidifying the binary opposition between good and evil that serves to maintain Jehovah's control.

The narrative control exerted over the interpretation of dreams and omens represents another dimension of this deception. Dream interpretation, a common practice in many ancient cultures, provided a pathway to understanding the unseen world and personal experiences. However, the Jehovah's narrative often portrays dreams as either divinely inspired pronouncements reinforcing its authority or deceitful manifestations of demonic influence, subtly undermining alternative interpretations. Similarly, omens, typically understood as messages from the natural world or ancestors, become signs of divine favor or disfavor, reinforcing the idea that understanding the world is dependent upon Jehovah's arbitrary interpretations. This manipulation of seemingly neutral sources of knowledge serves to reinforce the power imbalance between Jehovah and humanity.

The study of ancient myths and symbols reveals the subtle ways in which narratives are constructed and manipulated to serve particular interests. By understanding how seemingly benign stories and symbols have been reinterpreted to support Jehovah's narrative, we begin to see the manipulative nature of power structures. The re-examination of these ancient narratives is not about rejecting them entirely but about recognizing the layers of meaning concealed beneath the surface. It involves engaging with these narratives critically, understanding their historical context and the ways in which they have been selectively interpreted to consolidate power and suppress alternative perspectives. This critical understanding is essential for discerning truth from deception, allowing for a more nuanced and liberated spiritual experience. This is not an easy task, as the layers of deception are deeply ingrained, but it is a necessary one, allowing us to recover the true meaning behind the myths and symbols that have shaped human culture and belief systems for millennia. The process requires patience, diligence, and a willingness to challenge established narratives, recognizing that the truth often lies buried beneath layers of carefully constructed illusion. By peeling back those layers, we gain a clearer understanding of the past, present, and future implications of religiously motivated manipulation. The ultimate goal is to reclaim our spiritual autonomy, to liberate ourselves from the narratives that have been imposed upon us, and to forge our own path towards a deeper, more authentic spiritual understanding.

Archaeological Anomalies. Physical Evidence of the Extraterrestrial Presence

The preceding discussion explored the manipulative power embedded within religious narratives, subtly altering the meaning and impact of ancient myths and symbols. This manipulation, however, is not confined to the realm of textual interpretation. A compelling argument can be made that the influence extends into the physical world, manifesting in archaeological anomalies that challenge conventional explanations and suggest a far more complex history of human interaction, potentially involving extraterrestrial presence.

The most frequently cited examples of such anomalies include objects and structures that demonstrate an advanced level of technological sophistication seemingly incongruent with the accepted timeline of human technological development. The Antikythera mechanism, a complex astronomical calculator dating back to the 1st century BCE, is a prime example. Its intricate gears, precisely engineered to predict celestial movements, far surpass the technological capabilities attributed to that era. While some scholars argue that its complexity could be the result of lost or forgotten technological know-how within the ancient Greek world, the sheer sophistication of the device raises questions that remain unanswered within a purely terrestrial technological framework. The precision of its engineering, its ability to predict eclipses and planetary positions with remarkable accuracy, and its miniaturization, all point to a level of understanding and execution that is remarkably advanced for its time. Could this device represent the remnants of a lost technology, possibly influenced by external sources? Or is it a product of a previously underestimated level of ancient Greek ingenuity, the extent of which is still being unraveled?

Similarly, the Nazca Lines of Peru, colossal geoglyphs etched into the desert landscape, present a fascinating enigma. Their scale and complexity, visible only from the air, have led to speculation about their purpose and origin. While theories abound, ranging from astronomical calendars to ritualistic pathways, the lack of conclusive evidence and the precision required to create these intricate designs fuel ongoing debate. Could their creation have been aided by advanced technology, perhaps even guidance from an outside source? Or could a deeper understanding of the ancient Nazca civilization's societal structure, beliefs, and knowledge reveal a previously unrecognized level of ingenuity?

The Puma Punku site in Bolivia, part of the Tiwanaku complex, offers another compelling example. The precision of the stonework, the intricate joins between massive blocks of stone, and the sophisticated techniques used to shape and transport these immense structures continue to baffle archaeologists. The uniformity of the stone blocks, some weighing many tons, and the accuracy of their fit suggest a level of technological prowess far beyond the capabilities usually associated with the civilization that is credited with their creation. Some researchers have proposed that advanced tools and techniques, perhaps employing sound or other unknown technologies, were used to achieve such perfection. Could extraterrestrial intervention have played a role in constructing these remarkable structures, or does a closer examination of the site and of surviving Tiwanaku culture reveal as-yet-undiscovered building methods?

Moreover, the recurring discovery of Out-of-Place Artifacts further fuels this debate. These are objects found in geological strata inconsistent with their presumed age and technological sophistication. For instance, the discovery of metallic objects embedded in ancient rocks, or advanced tools found in geological formations dating back millions of years, challenges conventional understandings of human history and technological progression. While skeptics often attribute such findings to misidentification, contamination, or inaccurate dating, the persistence of these anomalies continues to generate questions that remain unanswered. Could some Artifacts represent evidence of ancient interactions with extraterrestrial civilizations, technologies far exceeding those of the surrounding cultures, and left behind long before the emergence of any known civilization? Or do these discoveries require a complete reevaluation of our assumptions about Earth's geological history and the timeline of human technological development?

It's crucial to acknowledge the inherent difficulties in interpreting archaeological evidence. Dating techniques are not infallible; there is always the possibility of contamination or misinterpretation. Moreover, the absence of clear, definitive evidence doesn't necessarily disprove the possibility of extraterrestrial involvement; it simply highlights the limitations of our current understanding and the need for further investigation. Many alternative explanations are plausible and deserve careful consideration. For example, the advanced capabilities of certain ancient cultures might have been lost or forgotten over time, leading to an underestimation of their technological achievements.

However, the sheer number and variety of these anomalies, considered together, present a challenging puzzle. Dismissing them all as isolated occurrences or simple misinterpretations requires a significant leap of faith. A more nuanced approach involves acknowledging the limitations of current knowledge while remaining open to the possibility of unconventional explanations, including the potential influence of extraterrestrial factors. The focus should not be on definitively proving extraterrestrial involvement but rather on engaging with the evidence objectively, considering all possible explanations, and encouraging further investigation.

Further complicating the picture are the various claims of ancient astronaut theorists and other researchers who interpret these anomalies through the lens of extraterrestrial intervention. While their enthusiasm is commendable, it's essential to approach their claims with a critical eye, distinguishing between well-documented archaeological findings and speculative interpretations. Some proponents overreach in their conclusions, relying on anecdotal evidence or unsubstantiated claims, ultimately undermining the credibility of their arguments. A rigorous and balanced approach is necessary, separating fact from speculation and employing the scientific method to analyze the available evidence.

The challenge lies in navigating the fine line between healthy skepticism and unwarranted dismissal. A truly scientific approach requires a willingness to question established paradigms and explore unconventional hypotheses while maintaining a commitment to rigorous methodology and evidence-based reasoning. It is only through such an approach that we can hope to unravel the mysteries surrounding these archaeological anomalies and gain a clearer understanding of our own past. The pursuit of knowledge, particularly when exploring controversial and potentially paradigm-shifting discoveries, demands patience, open-mindedness, and a rigorous adherence to the principles of scientific inquiry. Only through a sustained and meticulous approach can we hope to uncover the truth, whatever that truth may be. The potential implications are far-reaching, impacting our understanding not only of history and technology but also of our place in the cosmos. This ongoing exploration underscores the importance of continuous research, critical thinking, and a commitment to unraveling the mysteries of our past, regardless of the complexity or challenge involved. The quest for understanding continues, and the answers might lie in the careful examination of seemingly insignificant details, the re-evaluation of accepted historical narratives, and the courage to explore unconventional hypotheses.

The Role of Secret Societies. Guardians of the Truth or Agents of Deception

The preceding discussion highlighted the perplexing anomalies within archaeological discoveries, prompting questions about our understanding of the past and the potential for previously unknown influences on human history. This naturally leads us to consider the role of secret societies, organizations often shrouded in secrecy and intrigue, whose activities and influence have been the subject of much speculation and debate for centuries. Did these societies act as guardians of esoteric knowledge, preserving truths intentionally obscured from the public eye? Or were they instruments of deception, manipulating narratives and controlling the flow of information to maintain their power and influence? The answer, as with many historical questions, is likely nuanced, with a spectrum of intentions and actions rather than a simple dichotomy.

One of the central challenges in assessing the role of secret societies lies in the nature of secrecy itself. By definition, their activities are hidden from public scrutiny, making it difficult to ascertain their true motives and impact. Historical accounts are often biased, incomplete, or deliberately misleading, making objective analysis a significant undertaking. Much of what we know about these groups comes from fragmented records, rumors, and interpretations of their symbols and rituals, often colored by the perspectives and agendas of those who record them.

Let us consider the Freemasons, arguably one of the most well-known and widely studied secret societies. Their origins are shrouded in mystery, with various claims tracing their lineage back to ancient guilds of stonemasons or even further, to mystical traditions of the distant past. Their elaborate rituals, symbolic language, and hierarchical structure have fueled numerous interpretations, ranging from benign fraternal organizations to shadowy groups wielding immense power and influence over world events. Some researchers point to the Masonic symbolism's potential connection to ancient Egyptian or even more ancient sources, suggesting that their knowledge is a direct line to an earlier, hidden tradition.

Others dismiss such claims as fanciful speculation, emphasizing the largely secular, philanthropic activities of many Masonic lodges throughout history.

Similarly, the Knights Templar, a medieval military order, hold a significant place in popular imagination, often portrayed as guardians of sacred secrets and repositories of ancient knowledge. Their sudden and brutal suppression by King Philip IV of France in 1307, leading to the deaths and imprisonment of many of their members, has fueled countless conspiracy theories, suggesting that their true power and knowledge were far more significant than officially acknowledged. Their supposed discovery of the Ark of the Covenant or other sacred artifacts, along with their connection to early banking and finance, add to their enigmatic aura and have been cited as evidence of their involvement in maintaining and controlling the flow of crucial historical information. While the historical records offer a more prosaic explanation for their demise – primarily revolving around political and economic conflicts – the enduring mystery surrounding the Knights Templar continues to fuel speculation about their true role and hidden purposes.

The Rosicrucians, a more elusive group, emerged in the 17th century, leaving behind a cryptic legacy of alchemical and mystical writings. Their symbolic language and elusive nature have made them a source of endless fascination for scholars and esoteric researchers. The Rosicrucian manifestos, filled with enigmatic symbolism and esoteric teachings, hint at a deeper understanding of the universe and human nature, perhaps drawing upon older traditions preserved through generations of secretive practice. However, their actual influence on historical events remains a matter of much debate, with some historians emphasizing their limited practical impact, while others suggest a more significant, albeit indirect, role in shaping intellectual and philosophical currents.

Beyond these prominent groups, countless other secret societies, both large and small, have existed throughout history, their activities largely obscured from public view. Some claim to have guarded ancient wisdom and esoteric knowledge, passing it down through generations of initiates.

Others have been implicated in political conspiracies and power struggles, manipulating events behind the scenes to advance their own agendas.

The connection to ancient mysteries frequently involves the interpretation of religious narratives and symbols. Secret societies, some argue, act as custodians of ancient wisdom, interpreting and preserving knowledge lost or deliberately suppressed throughout the ages. The symbolism embedded within their rituals and ceremonies could be seen as a coded language, carrying layers of meaning only accessible to those initiated into their mysteries. However, it is important to be critical here. The interpretation of symbolism is inherently subjective, and often prone to exaggeration and misinterpretation. What might appear to be a carefully crafted message revealing profound truths to the initiated may be no more than a coincidence or a reflection of prevailing cultural beliefs and practices.

It is also crucial to acknowledge that many secret societies, in fact, had more mundane motivations. Some provided social networks and mutual support to their members, offering a sense of community and shared identity. Others served as fronts for political activism or social reform, using secrecy as a means of protection from persecution. The line between legitimate social groups and conspiratorial organizations is often blurred, making definitive judgments challenging.

The question of whether secret societies have acted as guardians of truth or agents of deception is ultimately a complex one, with no easy answers. Their histories are riddled with ambiguities, and their actions often shrouded in secrecy. The narratives surrounding these groups are frequently embellished by myth and legend, and the available evidence is often fragmentary and subject to interpretation. A comprehensive evaluation requires a balanced and critically discerning approach, capable of distinguishing between genuine historical evidence and the imaginative embellishments that often surround these powerful groups. Instead of viewing them as monolithic entities with singular goals, a more nuanced perspective considers the diversity of motives and actions among the various societies and their members throughout history. The search for truth, in this context, requires an unflinching examination of both the potential for concealment and the possibility of preservation of ancient knowledge, weighing the evidence carefully and recognizing the limits of what we can definitively know. Only through this methodical approach can we hope to approach a clearer understanding of their roles throughout history. The persistent allure of these secretive organizations continues to shape our understanding of power, knowledge, and the enduring human fascination with mystery, ultimately contributing to a complex and ever-evolving narrative.

Connecting the Dots. A Synthesis of Evidence

The preceding sections have explored various lines of evidence suggesting a deliberate manipulation of historical narratives, focusing specifically on the portrayal of Yahweh/Jehovah in religious texts. We have examined discrepancies in archaeological findings, the enigmatic roles of secret societies, and the inherent ambiguities within religious scriptures themselves. Now, it is time to connect these seemingly disparate threads, weaving them into a coherent tapestry that reveals a more complex and potentially unsettling picture of humanity's past and its relationship with the divine.

One of the key inconsistencies lies in the stark contrast between the image of a benevolent, all-powerful deity presented in mainstream religious interpretations and the actions attributed to Jehovah in the biblical narrative. The Old Testament, particularly, depicts a deity capable of immense cruelty and capriciousness, inflicting devastating punishments on entire populations for seemingly minor transgressions. The stories of the flood, the destruction of Sodom and Gomorrah, and the numerous instances of divinely sanctioned violence paint a picture far removed from the compassionate and merciful God often invoked in modern religious discourse. This discrepancy raises questions about the selective presentation of religious narratives and the potential for deliberate omissions or alterations of original texts.

The archaeological evidence, as discussed earlier, further complicates this picture. The lack of concrete historical corroboration for many biblical events, combined with the discovery of older, potentially antecedent, religious traditions, points to a possible rewriting or reshaping of religious history to serve specific agendas. The inconsistencies between the archaeological record and the biblical account cannot be simply dismissed as minor inaccuracies. Instead, they suggest a more deliberate manipulation of historical narratives to create a specific theological and political framework.

Consider, for instance, the narrative of the Exodus. While the biblical account describes a mass exodus of enslaved Israelites from

Egypt, leaving a significant mark on history, there is scant independent archaeological evidence to support this narrative on the scale described. Some scholars argue that the Exodus, as depicted in the Bible, is a highly embellished or even entirely mythical account, designed to establish the Israelites' identity and claim to the Promised Land. This does not necessarily mean that no migration or liberation event occurred; it suggests that the biblical account is a selective and potentially manipulated version of historical events. Moreover, the lack of definitive archaeological confirmation does not automatically invalidate the story's spiritual or symbolic significance for believers. However, it does challenge the literal truthfulness of the account and highlights the potential for religious narratives to be shaped by political and ideological factors.

This brings us to the role of secret societies, whose influence on the shaping of religious narratives may have been far more significant than traditionally acknowledged. These organizations, often operating in secrecy, had access to ancient knowledge and traditions, including religious and spiritual practices, potentially pre-dating and even conflicting with the dominant religious frameworks. They could have played a crucial role in either preserving alternative interpretations of religious history or manipulating the existing narratives to serve their own purposes. The nature of secrecy inherently makes it difficult to fully ascertain the extent of this influence; however, the recurring presence of esoteric symbolism and cryptic rituals in many religious traditions suggests a possible connection to these clandestine groups. Their supposed access to ancient texts and traditions offers a possible explanation for the discrepancies and inconsistencies within the canonical religious texts.

The textual analysis of religious scriptures itself reveals further evidence of potential manipulation. Close scrutiny of the biblical text shows inconsistencies, contradictions, and editorial changes that point to a layered, evolving narrative rather than a single, divinely inspired account. The inclusion and exclusion of specific passages, the variation in interpretations across different translations, and the alterations made over centuries of scribal transmission all contribute to the complexity and ambiguity of the text. This raises questions about who controlled the process of textual transmission and what specific ideological or political agendas were at play. The sheer diversity of interpretations, particularly concerning the nature of Jehovah, highlights the inherent flexibility and malleability of religious narratives. The capacity of religious texts to be interpreted and reinterpreted across different historical periods and cultural contexts does not invalidate their spiritual significance for many believers, but it does highlight the human agency involved in their transmission and interpretation.

The synthesis of this evidence points toward a more nuanced understanding of the relationship between religious narratives, history, and power. The seemingly benevolent image of Jehovah presented in mainstream religious discourse is significantly challenged when confronted with the alternative interpretations supported by the accumulated evidence. The inconsistencies in archaeological findings, the potential manipulation by secret societies, and the inherent ambiguities of the biblical text suggest that the canonical religious narratives, particularly concerning Jehovah, may be a carefully constructed story, deliberately shaped to suit specific political and ideological agendas. The narrative of a loving and merciful God might obscure a more complex reality, a historical reality involving the suppression of alternative narratives and the deliberate creation of a religious framework designed to serve the interests of those in power.

It is important to note that this alternative narrative does not necessarily diminish the spiritual significance of religious faith for individuals. The belief in a divine presence remains a matter of personal conviction, not necessarily subject to the constraints of historical verification. However, by critically examining the historical and textual evidence, we can gain a deeper appreciation of the complexity of religious narratives and the role of power in shaping our understanding of the divine. The conclusion that emerges from this integrated analysis is not a simple condemnation of religious faith but rather an invitation to a more nuanced and historically conscious engagement with religious texts and traditions. The journey of faith remains personal and profoundly meaningful, but the understanding of its historical context is enriched by a critical, multidisciplinary approach. By acknowledging the possibility of manipulation and distortion within religious narratives, we can move towards a more informed and responsible engagement with the past, present, and future of religious belief. The pursuit of truth, in this realm, requires a willingness to confront uncomfortable truths and to acknowledge the limitations of our knowledge. The story of Jehovah, as presented in religious texts, may not be the full or unbiased account, and recognizing this opens up a new level of understanding of the complexities of religious faith and its relationship with power. The exploration of religious narratives must always involve both faith and critical analysis, creating a space for both personal belief and historical scrutiny. Only through such a balanced approach can we hope to achieve a more truthful and complete understanding of humanity's spiritual journey.

REFLECTION: *If the flood really happened, why can't we find the Ark?*

Genesis 8:4. On the seventeenth day of the seventh month, the ark came to rest on the mountains of Ararat.

Chapter 3
The Psychological Impact of Belief

The Power of Belief. How Jehovah Manipulated Human Psychology

Building upon the preceding analysis of historical discrepancies and potential manipulations within religious narratives, we now delve deep into the potent psychological mechanisms through which belief systems, specifically the Jehovah-centric system of the Old Testament, exert their influence. The assertion is not that belief itself is inherently manipulative, but rather that the specific construction and deployment of the Jehovah narrative leveraged deeply ingrained psychological vulnerabilities for purposes of social control and the maintenance of power structures.

One fundamental aspect is the exploitation of our inherent need for meaning and purpose. Humans are not simply biological entities; we are meaning-making creatures. We desire to understand our place in the universe, the reasons behind suffering, and the ultimate destiny of our lives. Religious systems, including the Jehovah-based one, offer comprehensive narratives that provide answers to these existential questions, often promising comfort and solace in the face of uncertainty. This "meaning-making" function is deeply satisfying, and the emotional reward reinforces the acceptance of the associated beliefs and practices, even in the face of contradictory evidence or ethical quandaries. The narrative of Jehovah's plan, from creation to judgment, provides a framework for understanding life's complexities, regardless of whether this framework aligns with historical accuracy or rational scrutiny. The inherent human desire for coherence and understanding becomes a fertile ground for the cultivation of belief.

Furthermore, the Jehovah narrative taps into our innate fear of the unknown and the unpredictable. The depiction of Jehovah as an all-powerful, all-knowing, and often wrathful deity instills a sense of awe and even terror. This fear, though, is not necessarily negative within the context of the religious framework; it acts as a powerful motivator for obedience and conformity. The promise of divine reward and the threat of divine punishment are effective tools for maintaining social order and reinforcing adherence to established norms. The detailed descriptions of divine retribution in the Old Testament, such as the destruction of Sodom and Gomorrah, serve as potent warnings, deeply influencing the behavior of believers and fostering a climate of fear that solidifies the authority of the religious system. This mechanism is not unique to the Jehovah narrative; many religious systems utilize similar approaches, exploiting the primal fear of divine wrath to maintain control. However, the starkness and frequency of such depictions in the Old Testament warrant special attention in this analysis.

Another crucial psychological element is the exploitation of our need for belonging and social connection. Religious communities offer a sense of identity, belonging, and shared purpose. The shared beliefs, rituals, and practices create a powerful sense of community, providing individuals with a social support network and a sense of belonging that can be deeply fulfilling. Within the Jehovah-centric system, this sense of community is reinforced through the emphasis on communal worship, shared scripture, and the establishment of clear hierarchies within the religious structure. This fosters conformity and strengthens the system's ability to maintain control. The fear of exclusion or rejection from the community serves as another potent incentive for maintaining adherence to the prescribed beliefs and practices, even when these may conflict with personal values or rational judgment. The psychological need for social acceptance and belonging provides a potent mechanism for the preservation of religious norms, transcending simple faith.

In addition to these fundamental human needs, the Jehovah narrative subtly exploits cognitive biases. Confirmation bias, the tendency to favor information that confirms existing beliefs, plays a significant role. Believers are likely to interpret ambiguous events or information in a way that supports their existing faith, reinforcing their belief in the divine power of Jehovah. This self-perpetuating loop strengthens the hold of the religious narrative, making it increasingly resistant to alternative perspectives or conflicting evidence. The very act of seeking out and interpreting scripture, even contradictory scripture, is framed within the context of the pre-existing belief system, furthering confirmation bias. This makes critical analysis of religious texts particularly difficult; the framework of belief colors the lens through which the text is viewed.

Further, the Jehovah narrative cleverly utilizes the availability heuristic, the tendency to overestimate the likelihood of events that are easily recalled. Vivid and emotionally charged stories of divine intervention, punishment, or miraculous events, as recounted in the Old Testament, become readily available in memory, disproportionately influencing judgments about the likelihood of such events occurring again. This makes the possibility of divine intervention seem more probable than it might be based on objective evidence. The emphasis on dramatic events, coupled with the human tendency to focus on emotionally salient information, reinforces the belief in the active and interventional nature of Jehovah. Such narrative construction becomes an effective tool in shaping beliefs and guiding behavior.

Moreover, the Jehovah system utilizes groupthink, a psychological phenomenon where the desire for group harmony overrides critical thinking and independent judgment. Within the community of believers, dissenting opinions or critical inquiries are often discouraged or suppressed, reinforcing conformity and maintaining the consensus view. The emphasis on communal harmony and obedience to religious authority discourages the expression of doubt or skepticism. The resulting group cohesion further reinforces the acceptance of the narrative, even when it is incongruent with broader rational or historical perspectives. This dynamic prevents internal challenges and criticism of the religious authority and its interpretations.

The concept of divine authority and the inherent ambiguity within sacred texts create further opportunities for manipulation. The claim of divinely inspired authority, particularly in the context of the Old Testament, creates an environment where the texts are presented as immutable and unchallengeable truths. This effectively shuts down critical inquiry, discouraging examination of historical inconsistencies and internal contradictions within the narrative itself. The potential for multiple interpretations, while presented as evidence of depth and richness, can also be employed to deflect criticism; inconvenient passages can be reinterpreted or simply ignored in favor of ones that support the desired outcome. This flexible interpretation prevents the narrative from becoming static and vulnerable to refutation.

Finally, the psychological impact of indoctrination, especially from a young age, is a powerful factor in maintaining belief in the Jehovah narrative. Early exposure to religious teachings shapes the individual's worldview and cognitive framework, making it more difficult to question or reject those teachings later in life. This inculcation of religious beliefs from an early age serves to deeply embed them into the personality and value system of the individual, making questioning or abandoning the faith a challenging prospect. The ingrained nature of these beliefs, instilled before critical thinking abilities are fully developed, strengthens the power of the narrative over the life of the believer.

In conclusion, while religious belief itself is a complex and deeply personal phenomenon, the specific construction and deployment of the Jehovah narrative within the Old Testament demonstrate a sophisticated understanding and utilization of human psychology. By tapping into fundamental psychological needs and vulnerabilities, employing cognitive biases, and leveraging social dynamics, the narrative achieved and maintained a level of control and influence far beyond that attributable to faith alone. This is not to deny the genuine faith and spiritual experiences of believers, but to understand the nuanced and potentially manipulative mechanisms through which power structures historically exploited human psychology to shape and control religious narratives. The critical examination of these mechanisms is crucial for a more informed and responsible engagement with both religious texts and the historical forces that shaped them. Understanding this interplay between human psychology and religious authority allows for a more nuanced understanding of the history of religion and its ongoing impact on human societies.

REFLECTION: Why are the questions, the doubt, the seeking of clarification not welcomed at religious systems, despite those systems saying that it is ok to ask questions?

The Creation of Fear and Control. Maintaining the Status Quo

The narrative of Jehovah, as presented in the Old Testament, is not simply a recounting of historical events; it is a carefully constructed narrative designed to instill fear and maintain control. This is not to diminish the genuine faith and spiritual experiences of believers, but rather to analyze the sophisticated techniques employed to leverage human psychology for the consolidation and preservation of power. The threat of divine retribution, explicitly and implicitly woven into the fabric of the text, serves as a potent instrument of control, shaping behavior and suppressing dissent. The detailed descriptions of punishments meted out by Jehovah – from the flood that wiped out humanity to the destruction of Sodom and Gomorrah – are not merely historical accounts but cautionary tales, vividly illustrating the consequences of disobedience and challenging the established order. These narratives, passed down through generations, instilled a deep-seated fear of divine wrath, making obedience to religious authorities and adherence to prescribed norms paramount for survival, both spiritual and, within the context of theocratic societies, physical.

This manipulation of fear extends beyond the explicit threats of divine punishment. The very ambiguity inherent within the Old Testament texts provided opportunities for selective interpretation and the reinforcement of existing power structures. Ambiguous passages could be interpreted in a variety of ways, depending on the needs and goals of those in power. Those in positions of authority, often the priestly class or religious leaders, could then utilize these interpretations to justify actions ranging from the subjugation of other groups to the perpetuation of social inequalities. This ambiguity, rather than being a flaw, served as a powerful tool, allowing for flexible adaptation to changing circumstances while maintaining a facade of divinely ordained authority.

The emphasis on divine omnipotence and omniscience further reinforced the sense of vulnerability and dependence on Jehovah, and subsequently on those who claimed to interpret his will. The concept of an all-seeing, all-knowing, and ultimately unforgiving God fosters a climate of constant surveillance and self-censorship. Individuals become more inclined to self-regulate their behavior, adhering to strict codes of conduct, not only out of faith but also out of a deeply ingrained fear of divine judgment. This internalized control is arguably more effective than any external force, creating a self-perpetuating system of obedience.

The use of fear also functioned to suppress dissent and critical inquiry. Any challenge to the established religious dogma could be framed as an act of rebellion against Jehovah himself, incurring the wrath not only of the religious leadership but also, and more significantly, of the divine. This effectively silenced alternative perspectives, creating an environment where conformity was rewarded and deviation was met with ostracization, or worse. The historical consequences of this suppression of dissent are evident in various instances where religious belief was used to justify persecution, violence, and oppression. The Inquisition, the Crusades, and countless other historical events serve as stark reminders of the destructive potential of religious narratives when they are used to maintain power and control through fear.

The concept of divinely ordained authority, meticulously crafted throughout the Old Testament, plays a pivotal role in maintaining the status quo. The portrayal of Jehovah as the ultimate lawgiver, the sole source of moral authority, rendered any secular or alternative power structures illegitimate. This effectively centralized power in the hands of those claiming to represent God's will, justifying their actions and decisions with divine mandate. This legitimization of authority through a divine claim is a potent mechanism for social control, precluding any challenge to their power based on secular or rational grounds.

Furthermore, the historical context of the Old Testament's creation and dissemination must be considered. The narratives were often created and disseminated in societies characterized by hierarchical social structures, with limited access to information and education. The power dynamic between religious leaders and the general populace was often profoundly unequal, further enhancing the efficacy of fear as a tool for control. Within this environment, the religious narrative could be manipulated to reinforce and justify existing social hierarchies, with those in power portraying themselves as divinely appointed guardians of order and morality.

The construction and dissemination of these narratives also employed sophisticated rhetorical techniques. The use of vivid imagery, emotionally charged language, and repeated pronouncements of divine wrath served to deeply embed the fear of Jehovah into the collective consciousness. These narratives became ingrained in the cultural fabric, passed down through generations and reinforced through rituals, practices, and social interactions. This multi-faceted approach ensured the long-term efficacy of this system of control, weaving fear into the very foundation of societal norms and beliefs.

Beyond the overt threats, the Old Testament also uses subtle forms of psychological manipulation to maintain its power. The promise of divine reward in the afterlife, while seemingly offering solace and hope, simultaneously acts as a form of control. The promise of eternal life in paradise serves as a potent incentive to adhere to religious doctrine, even when faced with difficult choices or ethical dilemmas. This carrot-and-stick approach – the threat of eternal damnation coupled with the promise of eternal bliss – is a highly effective technique for shaping behavior and maintaining conformity.

The narrative also strategically employed the technique of scapegoating. The identification of specific groups or individuals as enemies of Jehovah provided a convenient mechanism for channeling societal anxieties and frustrations. These scapegoats became targets of aggression and violence, further consolidating the power of those in control by diverting attention away from internal conflicts or systemic issues. This tactic served to unify the community against a common enemy, reinforcing the cohesion of the religious group and solidifying the authority of its leaders.

Moreover, the narrative structure itself fostered a sense of group identity and belonging, contributing to the maintenance of the system's power. The shared beliefs, rituals, and practices of the religious community created a strong sense of unity and solidarity, making it difficult for individuals to question the established order or deviate from the prescribed norms. The fear of ostracization or expulsion from the community, with its inherent support system and social connections, served as a powerful mechanism for social control. This sense of belonging, while fulfilling on an emotional level, also functioned as a form of psychological imprisonment, reinforcing the authority of the religious system.

In conclusion, the Jehovah narrative, as presented in the Old Testament, is not simply a religious text; it is a complex interplay of religious belief, historical context, and sophisticated psychological manipulation. The strategic use of fear and control, achieved through the employment of vivid imagery, ambiguous language, selective interpretation, scapegoating, and the fostering of group identity, allowed this narrative to achieve and maintain a level of power and influence that significantly transcends the realm of purely spiritual conviction. Understanding this dynamic is critical to analyzing the historical impact of religion and its continuing influence on human societies. The ability to discern between genuine faith and manipulative narratives is crucial for fostering a society characterized by informed consent, ethical decision-making, and the respectful engagement with both religious beliefs and historical power dynamics.

Reflection: The narrative of fear and punishment is almost the same used by the state. Fear, punishment and control to keep the Status Quo.

The Role of Ritual and Ceremony Reinforcing Belief and Control

The previous section explored the ways in which the Old Testament narrative, particularly the portrayal of Jehovah, employs psychological manipulation to establish and maintain control. We now turn our attention to the crucial role of ritual and ceremony in reinforcing this control and solidifying belief. Rituals and ceremonies are not merely symbolic acts; they are powerful tools that shape behavior, cultivate emotional responses, and solidify social structures. Within the context of the Old Testament's narrative, these practices serve as vital mechanisms for both reinforcing faith in Jehovah and maintaining the power of those who claim to represent His will.

The repetition inherent in ritual is a key component of its efficacy. Repetitive actions, chants, and prayers create a hypnotic effect, fostering a sense of trance-like immersion and enhancing suggestibility. This heightened suggestibility makes individuals more receptive to the religious narrative and less likely to question its underlying assumptions. The repetitive nature of religious practices, from the daily prayers to the annual festivals, creates a predictable and comforting rhythm in the lives of believers, reinforcing their adherence to the religious framework. This predictability is especially important in societies characterized by uncertainty and instability, offering a sense of order and security in an otherwise chaotic world.

Consider the Passover Seder, a central ritual in Jewish tradition. The meticulous reenactment of the Exodus story, generation after generation, serves not only as a remembrance of historical events but also as a powerful affirmation of religious identity and belief. Each element of the Seder – the symbolic foods, the readings from the Haggadah, the songs and blessings – contributes to a collective experience that strengthens faith and reinforces the narrative of divine intervention and liberation. The ritual itself becomes a conduit for transmitting the religious narrative and cultivating a sense of shared history and collective identity. The meticulous detail and structured format ensure consistency and conformity, minimizing opportunities for individual interpretation or deviation from the established norms.

The visceral nature of many religious rituals further enhances their psychological impact. The use of sensory experiences, such as incense, music, chanting, and physical movement, stimulates multiple senses, creating a powerful emotional response that goes beyond intellectual comprehension. These heightened emotional states make individuals more susceptible to suggestion and more readily accept the authority of religious leaders and the pronouncements of divine will. The emotional power of these rituals reinforces belief and fosters a sense of unity and solidarity among participants. This collective emotional experience strengthens the bonds of the community and reinforces its allegiance to the religious system.

Furthermore, religious ceremonies often involve dramatic enactments of religious narratives or symbolic representations of religious concepts. These dramatic representations transform abstract theological concepts into tangible experiences, making them more accessible and more emotionally engaging for the believer. This heightened emotional engagement strengthens the belief system and makes it less vulnerable to rational critique. The spectacle and grandeur of such ceremonies reinforce the power and authority of the religious system, further cementing its influence over the lives of its adherents. The visual and theatrical aspects are especially crucial in societies with limited access to literacy, where the oral tradition and visual representations play a far more significant role in transmitting religious knowledge and beliefs.

The social dimension of religious rituals is also critical to their efficacy. Participating in these ceremonies provides individuals with a sense of community and belonging, strengthening social bonds and reinforcing group identity. This sense of collective identity reinforces the authority of the religious leaders and makes it more difficult for individuals to challenge the established order. The fear of social exclusion and ostracism from the community serves as a powerful incentive to conform to the norms and expectations of the religious system. This social pressure is often far more effective than any form of overt coercion, ensuring long-term adherence to the religious framework.

The hierarchical structure of many religious rituals further reinforces the authority of religious leaders. These leaders often act as intermediaries between the deity and the congregation, controlling access to religious symbols, practices, and interpretations. The ritual itself becomes a demonstration of this authority, with the leaders acting as the central figures, directing the actions and interpreting the significance of the events. This reinforces the idea that religious leaders have a special connection to the divine, justifying their claim to authority and legitimizing their power. This power dynamic is reinforced through the ritual itself, creating a self-perpetuating cycle of authority and obedience.

In addition to the psychological manipulation inherent in the rituals themselves, religious ceremonies also serve as important tools for social control. Religious festivals, for example, often involve collective acts of devotion, which serve as powerful displays of allegiance to the religious system. These public demonstrations of faith reinforce social conformity and discourage any deviation from the established norms. The social pressure to participate in these events, coupled with the potential for social ostracism for non-participation, reinforces the system's control over the lives of its adherents. These large-scale events also serve as a demonstration of the power and reach of the religious system, further cementing its dominance within the social structure.

The use of sacred spaces and objects in religious rituals also contributes to their effectiveness. Sacred spaces, such as temples or churches, create a sense of awe and reverence, reinforcing the perceived power of the religious system. The use of sacred objects, such as relics or icons, creates a tangible connection between the believer and the divine, further enhancing the emotional impact of religious practices. These tangible elements enhance the ritual's effectiveness and contribute to the overall power of the religious system. The controlled access to these spaces and objects further reinforces the authority of the religious leaders.

Moreover, religious rituals often incorporate elements of sacrifice, whether it be animal sacrifice or the symbolic sacrifice of time, effort, or personal desires. This act of sacrifice reinforces the notion of dependence on the divine and strengthens the bonds between the believer and the religious system. The act of giving something up, whether it is material or symbolic, increases the value placed on the religious system and demonstrates a commitment to its tenets. This sense of commitment strengthens the believer's identity within the religious community and reinforces the authority of the religious leaders.

Finally, it's essential to consider the enduring nature of religious traditions. Religious rituals, passed down through generations, create a sense of continuity and tradition, reinforcing the legitimacy and stability of the religious system. These traditions create a sense of cultural heritage and provide a sense of identity that transcends individual lives. This sense of continuity is crucial for maintaining the power of the religious system, as it allows the system to maintain its influence across generations. The consistent transmission of these rituals ensures the continued perpetuation of belief and the maintenance of the system of power. The weight of history, combined with the powerful psychological effects of the rituals, ensures the long-term efficacy of this form of social control.

In conclusion, religious rituals and ceremonies are far more than symbolic acts. They are powerful tools for shaping behavior, reinforcing beliefs, and maintaining control. The intricate interplay of repetition, sensory stimulation, emotional engagement, social dynamics, hierarchical structures, sacred spaces, sacrifice, and generational transmission creates a powerful system of social control that significantly transcends the purely spiritual. Understanding the psychological mechanisms at work within these rituals is crucial to comprehending the historical and ongoing influence of religion on human societies. The Old Testament, with its elaborate rituals and ceremonies, provides a compelling case study in how religion can effectively utilize these mechanisms to establish and maintain power, ultimately shaping not only individual beliefs but also the broader social and political landscape.

REFLECTION: Time to do your own reflections.

The Suppression of Dissent. Maintaining the Illusion of Authority

The carefully constructed edifice of religious authority, as presented in the Old Testament, rests not only on the persuasive power of its narrative and the hypnotic influence of its rituals, but also on the systematic suppression of dissent. The narrative itself, while claiming divine inspiration, often depicts a God who brooks no contradiction and metes out swift and brutal punishment to those who question his commands or challenge his authority. This divine model of intolerance subtly yet powerfully shapes the behavior of those who claim to represent Jehovah's will on Earth. The threat of divine retribution, meticulously detailed in numerous passages, serves as a potent deterrent against open rebellion, fostering a climate of fear and self-censorship within the community.

The consequences of challenging the established religious order were often severe, ranging from social ostracism and economic ruin to imprisonment, torture, and even death. The Old Testament, while not explicitly detailing methods of systematic suppression, hints at the brutal realities of opposing religious authority. The stories of prophets facing persecution, the accounts of those punished for idolatry or heresy, and the descriptions of wars waged against those deemed enemies of God paint a picture of a society where dissent was not tolerated. These narratives serve not only to illustrate the potential consequences of opposition but also to reinforce the legitimacy of the existing power structures by demonizing those who dare to question them.

The suppression of dissent was not merely a matter of physical coercion; it was also a sophisticated psychological operation designed to maintain the illusion of Jehovah's absolute authority. This psychological manipulation involved a complex interplay of propaganda, censorship, and the manipulation of religious symbols and rituals. Religious leaders, acting as intermediaries between God and the people, controlled the interpretation of sacred texts, ensuring that any challenges to the prevailing orthodoxy were effectively neutralized. They often presented alternative interpretations as heretical, demonic, or a product of personal weakness or malevolence. This effectively isolated dissenting voices and delegitimized their perspectives in the eyes of the faithful.

The control over information was paramount. Access to the sacred texts, the means of their interpretation, and even the tools for literacy were often restricted to the priestly class or a small elite. This ensured that the religious narrative remained largely unchallenged and that alternative viewpoints were effectively suppressed. The lack of access to alternative interpretations effectively limited the possibility of independent thought and critical analysis of religious dogma. This control extended to the dissemination of religious teachings, limiting exposure to alternative perspectives and fostering a climate of intellectual conformity.

Furthermore, the manipulation of religious symbols and rituals played a crucial role in maintaining the illusion of authority. The elaborate ceremonies, described in detail within the Old Testament, served not only to reinforce faith but also to create a sense of awe and reverence for the religious leadership. The rituals themselves, often shrouded in mystery and symbolism, were carefully crafted to enhance the mystique of the priesthood and their connection to the divine. Any deviation from the prescribed rituals or their interpretation was often met with harsh punishment, thereby reinforcing the importance of unquestioning obedience.

The social consequences of dissent were as significant as the physical ones. The strong sense of community and belonging that the religious system fostered worked to suppress dissent through social pressure. Individuals who challenged the religious order were often ostracized, excommunicated, or even subjected to public shaming. The fear of social isolation and the loss of community support, coupled with the threat of divine retribution, ensured that most individuals conformed to the established norms. This form of social control was far more effective than overt coercion, as it operated on a subconscious level, subtly shaping the thoughts and actions of individuals without the need for explicit threats.

The narrative of chosen peoplehood, central to the Old Testament, also played a crucial role in suppressing dissent. By presenting the Israelites as a special, divinely chosen people with a unique covenant with God, the narrative instilled a strong sense of group identity and loyalty. This sense of belonging and specialness was used to justify actions that might otherwise be viewed as morally questionable, and to discourage questioning of the authority that was believed to be divinely ordained. Criticizing the religious system was tantamount to questioning the divine choice and the very identity of the community, rendering such criticism socially unacceptable and dangerous.

The development of a rigid legal system, often intertwined with religious law, further contributed to the suppression of dissent. This legal system, based on the interpretation of religious texts, prescribed penalties for a wide range of offences, including religious heresy. The intertwining of religious and legal authority ensured that challenges to the religious establishment faced legal consequences as well. This created a powerful mechanism for suppressing dissent, where challenging the religious order had both social and legal repercussions. This lack of separation between religious and secular power was essential for maintaining control.

The historical consequences of this suppression of dissent are profound. It led to periods of intellectual stagnation, the suppression of scientific inquiry, and the persecution of those who held differing beliefs. The narrative of a monolithic, unquestionable authority, meticulously constructed in the Old Testament, had a lasting impact on the societies that embraced it. The legacy of this suppression continues to influence religious and political structures even today, manifesting in various forms of intolerance, censorship, and the suppression of differing opinions.

Examining the Old Testament's narrative with a critical eye reveals not just a religious text, but also a powerful case study in the manipulation of belief and the suppression of dissent. The systematic methods used to ensure conformity, a mixture of divine threat, ritualistic indoctrination, social ostracism, and legal persecution, provide a stark reminder of the dangers of unchecked religious authority and the importance of critical thinking and the protection of freedom of expression. The narrative, while presented as divinely inspired, reveals itself as a potent tool for consolidating and maintaining power, a crucial element in understanding its enduring influence throughout history. The illusion of divine authority, meticulously maintained through the centuries, ultimately rests upon the suppression of those who would dare to challenge it. The historical record serves as a potent cautionary tale, highlighting the fragility of truth and the ever-present threat to free thought when power and faith become inextricably intertwined.

REFLECTION: The methods of excommunicate and social ostracism are effective and powerful methods to keep control.

Breaking Free from the Chains of Belief. A Path to Enlightenment

The insidious nature of belief systems, particularly those wielding the power of divine authority as portrayed in the Old Testament, lies not only in their overt pronouncements but also in their subtle psychological manipulation. The fear of divine retribution, the social ostracism threatened to dissenters, and the carefully constructed narratives designed to consolidate power; all these factors contributed to a climate of unquestioning obedience. However, the path towards genuine spiritual liberation, or what might be termed enlightenment, lies in breaking free from these chains of belief, in cultivating the capacity for critical thinking and self-awareness. This journey requires a conscious effort to dismantle the ingrained psychological mechanisms that perpetuate blind faith and acceptance.

The first step on this path involves a critical examination of the source material itself. The Old Testament, while revered as a sacred text by many, should be approached not as an infallible account of divine truth, but as a historical document reflecting the cultural and political realities of its time. Understanding the historical context, the power struggles, the social dynamics, and the political maneuvering that shaped the narrative is crucial to discerning the motivations behind the text. Reading the Old Testament with an awareness of the biases inherent in its creation, its potential propagandistic purpose, and its human authors allows for a more nuanced and detached understanding. This detached perspective is essential in combating the psychological power of the narrative.

The careful examination of the text must extend beyond its surface meaning to encompass a thorough analysis of its underlying assumptions, its implied values, and its inherent contradictions. The seemingly contradictory portrayals of God, for instance, a God of both love and wrath, of mercy and vengeance, reveal the complexity of the human experience projected onto the divine. Acknowledging these contradictions undermines the authority of a monolithic, all-powerful deity and paves the way for a more nuanced understanding of faith. This critical approach, rather than undermining faith, strengthens it by grounding it in reason and understanding rather than blind acceptance.

Moving beyond the textual analysis, the process of liberation necessitates a confrontation with personal biases and preconceived notions. Our upbringing, our cultural background, our social circles, all shape our beliefs and often subtly reinforce unquestioning adherence to established dogma. To break free from this psychological conditioning requires a conscious effort to identify and challenge our own biases. This is a difficult and sometimes painful process, requiring honest self-reflection and a willingness to confront uncomfortable truths about ourselves and our beliefs. Journaling, meditation, and engaging in open, honest dialogue with others who hold differing views can be invaluable tools in this process.

The development of critical thinking skills is paramount in escaping the psychological grip of unquestioning faith. Critical thinking involves the ability to analyze information objectively, to identify logical fallacies, to evaluate evidence, and to form reasoned conclusions. This is not about rejecting faith outright but rather about grounding it in a framework of reason and evidence. This involves learning to distinguish between verifiable facts and unsubstantiated claims, between reasoned arguments and emotional appeals. Engaging with diverse viewpoints, challenging one's assumptions, and seeking out evidence that contradicts one's beliefs are all essential components of critical thinking. This is not a rejection of faith but an evolution of it, a deepening and refining of one's beliefs through reason and analysis.

Cultivating self-awareness is inextricably linked to the development of critical thinking. Self-awareness involves a deep understanding of one's own thoughts, emotions, and motivations. By understanding how our beliefs shape our perceptions and actions, we can begin to identify the subtle ways in which our faith might be influencing our decisions and behavior. This increased self-awareness allows us to make more informed choices, free from the unconscious pressures of ingrained beliefs. Practices such as mindfulness meditation, introspection, and self-reflection can aid in this process of self-discovery. Understanding our biases, our motivations, and our emotional responses allows for a more objective assessment of our beliefs and their impact on our lives.

The path to enlightenment, as understood in this context, is not about discarding all religious beliefs but rather about transforming them. It is about moving from a position of unquestioning faith to one of informed, critical engagement. It is about replacing blind acceptance with reasoned understanding. This process involves recognizing the historical, cultural, and psychological factors that have shaped our beliefs and actively working to overcome the limitations they impose. The journey requires courage, honesty, and a commitment to intellectual and spiritual growth.

The freedom from the chains of belief is not an abandonment of spirituality but a deepening of it. By critically engaging with our faith, by confronting our biases, and by cultivating critical thinking and self-awareness, we can move beyond the limitations of rigid dogma and embrace a more nuanced, richer, and ultimately more authentic spiritual experience. This is a journey of self-discovery, a journey towards a more complete understanding of ourselves and our place in the world. It's a journey that requires constant questioning, rigorous self-examination, and a lifelong commitment to intellectual and spiritual growth. The reward, however, is a life lived with greater awareness, understanding, and freedom, a life informed not by blind faith but by conscious, informed belief.

This process is not easily achieved. It requires ongoing effort, a consistent commitment to self-reflection and a willingness to confront challenging ideas. It may necessitate reevaluating long-held beliefs and confronting the potential discomfort of intellectual and spiritual uncertainty. But the potential rewards are substantial: a greater understanding of oneself, a deeper connection with the world, and the freedom to live a life guided by reason, empathy, and a more authentic spiritual experience. This is not an abandonment of faith but a refinement, a deepening of understanding that replaces unquestioning obedience with conscious, informed participation in the spiritual journey. It is a journey of liberation, a path towards a more enlightened and fulfilling life, free from the limiting constraints of blind faith. The process itself is a testament to the power of human reason and the enduring quest for truth and understanding. It is a journey toward a richer, more authentic connection with oneself, others, and the divine, a path toward a more enlightened existence.

Finally, engaging with diverse perspectives and actively seeking out dissenting voices is crucial. The suppression of dissent is a hallmark of many belief systems, and actively engaging with different viewpoints fosters critical thinking and a broader understanding of the complexities of faith. By actively listening to and considering different interpretations, one can better understand the limitations of one's own perspective and broaden one's own understanding. This requires humility, a willingness to be challenged, and an open mind receptive to new information and perspectives. The goal is not necessarily to find agreement but to foster intellectual growth and a more nuanced understanding of the complexities of faith and belief. Only through open dialogue and critical engagement can one truly break free from the constraints of unchecked belief.

REFLECTION: Blind faith or conscious, informed belief? What do you prefer?

Chapter 4
The Alien Agenda

Jehovah's Ultimate Goals. What Does He Really Want

The preceding discussion highlighted the manipulative aspects of certain belief systems, particularly those rooted in the Old Testament. We explored the importance of critical thinking and self-awareness in breaking free from the psychological constraints of unquestioning faith. Now, let us delve into a more speculative, even controversial, realm: What are the ultimate goals of Jehovah, as depicted in the Old Testament, and what might these goals truly entail? This is a question that transcends mere theological interpretation and ventures into the territory of speculative fiction, employing the tools of critical analysis to explore unsettling possibilities.

One could argue that Jehovah's primary objective, as portrayed in the biblical narrative, is the establishment and maintenance of absolute power and control. This interpretation finds support in numerous passages that depict God's wrathful retribution against those who disobey or challenge his authority. The relentless emphasis on obedience, the fear-inducing narratives of divine punishment, and the strict adherence to codified laws all point towards a desire for unquestioning subservience. This isn't simply a matter of upholding morality; it's about consolidating power, ensuring the complete submission of humanity to a singular, all-powerful entity. This interpretation, while seemingly simplistic, resonates with numerous historical and contemporary power structures that rely on fear and coercion to maintain control. We see echoes of this in totalitarian regimes, cult leaderships, and even within certain religious institutions where dissent is met with ostracization or worse.

However, a deeper analysis might suggest a more nuanced and potentially more disturbing interpretation of Jehovah's motivations. The narrative of the Old Testament isn't solely about immediate control; it also hints at a grander, more long-term agenda. One could argue that Jehovah's actions, even his acts of apparent benevolence, serve a larger, perhaps even malevolent, purpose. This could involve a cosmic game of manipulation, a grand experiment in which humanity serves as unwitting pawns in a struggle for power that transcends our comprehension.

Let's consider the possibility of a divine "experiment," drawing inspiration from thought experiments in science fiction. Imagine Jehovah not as an omnipotent, omniscient being, but as a powerful entity experimenting with different forms of social control and religious structures. The Old Testament could then be seen as a record of this ongoing experiment, with different periods representing various stages of manipulation and control. The creation of humanity, the establishment of covenants, the introduction of laws, the cycles of reward and punishment, all could be viewed as components of this vast experiment, designed to observe human behavior under specific conditions. The resulting data, perhaps, informs the entity's long-term strategies, allowing for refinement and optimization of methods of control.

This speculative approach opens the door to contemplating potentially malevolent intentions. Perhaps Jehovah's ultimate goal isn't simply control but the systematic dehumanization of humanity, a gradual erosion of free will and independent thought, leading to a state of complete submission and unquestioning obedience. This is a chilling thought, but the narratives of the Old Testament, when viewed through this lens, reveal a pattern of behavior consistent with such a possibility. The constant testing of faith, the infliction of suffering, the manipulation of emotions, these actions could be seen as tools designed not to guide humanity towards spiritual growth, but to break its spirit and mold it into a pliable instrument.

Furthermore, the inconsistencies and contradictions within the Old Testament narratives could be interpreted as artifacts of this grand experiment. The conflicting portrayals of Jehovah, a God of both love and wrath, mercy and vengeance, might reflect an ongoing process of adjustment and refinement, a search for the most effective methods of manipulation and control. The seemingly arbitrary nature of divine pronouncements, the unpredictable shifts in mood and temperament, might be evidence of a learning process, an entity trying out different approaches to achieve its ultimate goals.

From another perspective, we could consider the possibility that Jehovah's actions are driven not by malice but by a form of misguided benevolence. Perhaps, from an alien perspective, Jehovah views humanity as a species prone to self-destruction, incapable of governing itself without external control. The strict rules, the harsh punishments, the insistence on obedience – all these might be interpreted as drastic measures to prevent humanity from obliterating itself. This would be a form of paternalistic control, justified not by a desire for power, but by a misplaced sense of responsibility.

However, this argument doesn't account for the inconsistencies and brutality within the narrative. Even under the guise of preventing self-destruction, the acts of genocide, the endorsement of slavery, and the countless instances of gratuitous violence remain disturbing and difficult to justify, even within a utilitarian framework.

To push this speculation further, we might draw upon the wealth of science fiction narratives exploring the concept of advanced alien civilizations interacting with primitive life forms. The human race could be viewed as a fascinating yet volatile species in the larger cosmic scheme of things, subject to observation and even manipulation by entities with vastly superior intellect and technology. In such a scenario, the Old Testament might not represent the direct intervention of a singular deity, but the actions of a complex, possibly technologically advanced civilization engaged in a vast and multifaceted project that stretches across millennia.

This perspective requires a suspension of disbelief, a willingness to consider narratives that challenge our traditional understanding of religion and spirituality. But by examining the biblical narrative through a science fiction lens, we gain a new perspective on the possible motivations behind Jehovah's actions, allowing us to question the nature of power, the boundaries of control, and the very definition of divinity. It allows us to move beyond the simplistic dichotomy of good versus evil and contemplate the far more complex and unsettling possibilities. It encourages us to analyze the narrative not merely for its religious implications, but for its psychological and sociological significance. It compels us to think critically about the relationship between power, belief, and control, and to question the very foundations of our belief systems.

The questions remain: What does Jehovah truly want? Is it simply control, a grand experiment, a misguided attempt at benevolent governance, or something else entirely, something far more sinister? The answers, inevitably, remain speculative, but the exploration of these possibilities compels us to examine critically the narratives that have shaped our world, forcing us to question the power structures that influence our lives and the very nature of faith itself. The process, however difficult and uncomfortable, is a crucial step towards a more enlightened and liberated understanding of ourselves, our beliefs, and our place in the universe. The journey of critical inquiry, the confrontation with unsettling possibilities, is a vital part of the path towards true spiritual liberation. Only through challenging the status quo, embracing uncomfortable truths, and examining our beliefs with rigorous intellectual honesty can we hope to attain a clearer, more authentic understanding of ourselves and the world around us. The ultimate goal, after all, is not blind faith, but informed and conscious engagement with the questions that shape our existence.

REFLECTION: Are we simply an Alien's experience?

The Manipulation of Resources. Jehovah's Control over Earth's Wealth

The previous exploration of Jehovah's potential motivations, ranging from a desire for absolute control to a misguided attempt at benevolent governance, leads us to a crucial, and arguably unsettling, aspect of the Old Testament narrative: the manipulation of resources. The biblical text, when examined through a critical lens, reveals a pattern of divine intervention that often results in the concentration of wealth and power within a select group, often those aligned with Jehovah's chosen people. This isn't merely a matter of divine reward; it suggests a deliberate, systemic manipulation of Earth's resources for the benefit of a specific agenda, an agenda that might be far more complex and self-serving than typically understood.

The narrative of the Exodus, for example, presents a compelling case study. The liberation of the Israelites from slavery in Egypt is often viewed as a triumph of faith and divine intervention. Yet, the subsequent narrative reveals a less celebrated aspect: the acquisition of vast wealth through the spoils of war and the appropriation of land previously occupied by other peoples. The Israelites' journey from oppressed slaves to a relatively prosperous nation is inextricably linked to the accumulation of resources – resources that weren't simply found but actively taken, often through acts of violence and displacement. The meticulous detail given to the division of the promised land, the allocation of resources, and the establishment of a hierarchical social structure reveals a pattern of controlled distribution, mirroring the mechanisms of power observed in many historical empires. This pattern raises questions about the true nature of Jehovah's benevolence. Was the liberation a purely altruistic act, or was it a calculated move to establish a powerful nation, a nation rich in both spiritual and material resources, strategically positioned for influence in the region?

This observation extends beyond the narrative of the Exodus. Throughout the Old Testament, we find repeated instances where Jehovah directs the allocation of resources, often favoring specific individuals or groups. The bestowal of wealth, the granting of victories in war, the promise of abundant harvests, these aren't simply rewards for piety; they are tools for consolidating power and influence. This divine intervention in the material world directly impacts the distribution of resources, creating a system where wealth and power become intertwined with religious authority.

The historical relationship between religious institutions and economic power further illuminates this dynamic. Throughout history, numerous religious organizations have amassed considerable wealth and influence, often wielding considerable control over the resources of their followers. The collection of tithes and offerings, the control of land and property, and the engagement in lucrative trade have all contributed to the accumulation of wealth within religious structures. While often justified as necessary for the maintenance of religious institutions and charitable works, these practices also served to reinforce the power of religious leaders and solidify their control over their communities.

This pattern suggests a broader, potentially disturbing, interpretation of Jehovah's role in the management of Earth's resources. If we consider the possibility of a deliberate, strategic manipulation of resources, the biblical narratives begin to appear less as tales of divine benevolence and more as accounts of a systematic consolidation of power. The Old Testament might then be seen not only as a religious text but also as a record of the strategic deployment of resources to achieve a specific socio-political outcome.

This perspective isn't about denouncing faith or denying the spiritual experiences of individuals. It's about applying critical analysis to the narrative, acknowledging the complexities and potential contradictions within it. It's about recognizing that the distribution of resources is a powerful mechanism for control, and that the narratives within the Old Testament reflect this reality.

Consider the concept of "divine right of kings," a theory that legitimized the rule of monarchs by asserting their authority was divinely ordained.

This theory wasn't simply a matter of spiritual legitimacy; it also provided a framework for the control of resources. The king, as God's representative on Earth, had the right to command the wealth and resources of the kingdom, often leading to lavish displays of power and the concentration of wealth within the ruling elite. The biblical narrative, with its emphasis on divinely ordained authority and the concentration of resources within the chosen people, mirrors this historical pattern, suggesting a deliberate connection between religious authority and economic power.

Furthermore, the Old Testament contains numerous instances of resource allocation driven by conflict and conquest. The conquest of Canaan, for example, is depicted as a divinely sanctioned event, resulting in the displacement of existing populations and the appropriation of their land and resources. This narrative presents a complex ethical dilemma. Is the acquisition of land and resources through conquest justified when sanctioned by divine authority? Such questions challenge our traditional understanding of divine justice and raise concerns about the potential for religious ideologies to be used to justify acts of violence and exploitation.

The historical record offers countless examples of this interplay between religious belief and the control of resources. The Crusades, fueled by religious zeal, resulted in the acquisition of vast wealth and territories, enriching religious institutions and expanding European influence. The Spanish conquest of the Americas, justified through a mixture of religious and imperial ambitions, led to the exploitation of indigenous populations and the plunder of vast resources. These historical events underscore the potential for religious ideologies to be instrumentalized for purposes of power and control, highlighting the need for a critical approach to religious texts that examines the relationship between faith, power, and the manipulation of resources.

The accumulation of wealth and the control of resources aren't merely incidental aspects of the Old Testament narrative; they are central to understanding the power dynamics depicted within the text. By examining the intricate ways in which Jehovah's actions influence the distribution of wealth and power, we gain a deeper understanding of the potential complexities and ambiguities within the religious narrative. It forces us to question the extent to which divine authority has been used to justify acts of exploitation and to consider the lasting consequences of intertwined religious and political power.

The implications of this perspective are profound. It challenges the traditional view of Jehovah as a benevolent deity, prompting us to consider the potential for manipulation and control embedded within the religious narrative. It compels us to examine the historical and contemporary relationship between religious institutions and economic power, urging us to engage in a critical assessment of the ways in which belief systems have been used to justify the unequal distribution of resources and the perpetuation of social hierarchies. Ultimately, this investigation opens a door to a more nuanced and critical understanding of religion, prompting us to consider the deeper, potentially unsettling implications of the stories we inherit and the beliefs that shape our world. The journey of questioning, of critically examining the narratives that have shaped our understanding of the world, is a crucial step toward achieving a more equitable and just future, a future where the manipulation of resources for the benefit of a select few is no longer accepted as the divinely ordained order of things.

REFLECTION: The Jehovah's manipulation paved the way to Status Quo.

The Control of Humanity. A Long-Term Strategy for Domination

The preceding analysis of Jehovah's manipulation of resources within the Old Testament framework suggests a broader, more chilling possibility: a long-term strategy for the control of humanity itself. If the concentration of wealth and power wasn't merely a consequence of divine favor, but a deliberate, calculated action, then what was the ultimate goal? What future did Jehovah envision for humanity, shaped by this meticulous management of earthly resources and the systematic allocation of power?

One potential interpretation is that Jehovah's actions reflect a desire for absolute, unwavering control. The chosen people, enriched and empowered by divine intervention, become a tool, a means to an end. Their prosperity isn't an act of benevolence but a strategic investment, fostering a loyal and powerful group capable of enforcing Jehovah's will upon the rest of humanity. The meticulous detailing of laws, commandments, and rituals within the Old Testament might then be viewed not only as spiritual guidance but as the intricate mechanisms of a complex control system, designed to maintain social order and ensure unwavering obedience. This system, meticulously crafted and divinely enforced, leaves little room for dissent or independent thought. The very structure of the religious narrative serves as a powerful instrument of control, shaping beliefs, behaviors, and ultimately, human destinies.

Consider the repeated emphasis on obedience and the dire consequences of disobedience throughout the Old Testament. The punishments for transgression are often severe, designed to instill fear and maintain compliance. This emphasis on obedience, combined with the carefully managed distribution of resources, suggests a system designed not for the free development of humanity but for its unwavering submission to a higher power. The narrative of the flood, for instance, can be interpreted not simply as divine judgment but as a decisive act of population control, eliminating those deemed unworthy or resistant to Jehovah's authority, leaving behind a more malleable population.

The implications of such a strategy are staggering. It suggests a view of humanity not as a partner in creation but as a resource to be managed, controlled, and ultimately, shaped according to a divine blueprint. This perspective raises ethical questions of unprecedented scale. If Jehovah's actions are interpreted through this lens, the narratives of the Old Testament shift from tales of benevolent guidance to accounts of a powerful entity manipulating the fate of humanity for its own inscrutable purposes. The very concept of free will becomes questionable, replaced by a deterministic view of history where human agency is constrained by divine design.

This interpretation, however, isn't necessarily inherently malevolent. A second potential motivation might stem from a misguided sense of benevolent paternalism. Jehovah, in this view, might believe himself to be acting in humanity's best interest, albeit through methods that would be considered oppressive and controlling by modern standards. The carefully managed distribution of resources could be seen as an attempt to prevent chaos and ensure the survival of humanity, even if this means sacrificing individual freedom and autonomy. The harsh punishments and the emphasis on obedience might be interpreted not as expressions of cruelty but as necessary measures to maintain order and prevent humanity from destroying itself.

This paternalistic perspective, however, presents its own set of problematic issues. It raises questions about the legitimacy of imposing one's will upon others, even under the guise of benevolent guidance. It highlights the dangers of assuming an omniscient perspective and the potential for such an assumption to lead to disastrous consequences. The imposition of a rigid social hierarchy, the control of information, and the suppression of dissenting voices, all characteristics of Jehovah's alleged long-term strategy, become mechanisms not of liberation but of oppression, regardless of the supposed intentions behind them. Even with the best of intentions, the resulting system remains profoundly authoritarian.

Examining the potential long-term consequences of Jehovah's actions requires considering various potential future scenarios. One possibility is the creation of a highly stratified society, rigidly controlled and governed by divinely ordained laws. This society, characterized by unwavering obedience and a strict adherence to religious dogma, might exist in a state of relative stability, but at the cost of individual freedom and creativity. Technological advancement might be stifled, replaced by a focus on maintaining the existing social order and preserving the power structure ordained by Jehovah. In this scenario, humanity might achieve a form of stability, but it would be a stability achieved through the suppression of individuality and the unwavering adherence to a predetermined societal structure.

Another possible consequence of Jehovah's actions could be the creation of a society that is perpetually on the brink of internal conflict. The manipulation of resources, the creation of a rigid social hierarchy, and the imposition of a strict religious code could lead to simmering tensions, potentially erupting into widespread violence and societal collapse. The very foundation of this society, built upon inequality and control, could prove inherently unstable, leading to cyclical periods of upheaval and conflict. In such a scenario, humanity would be trapped in a perpetual cycle of violence and instability, a direct consequence of the divinely imposed social order.

A third, more speculative possibility involves the eventual disillusionment of humanity with Jehovah's rule. As generations pass, and the mechanisms of control become increasingly apparent, resistance could emerge, potentially culminating in a widespread rejection of Jehovah's authority and a revolutionary overthrow of the existing power structure. This scenario would lead to a period of societal upheaval, potentially resulting in a new social order, one that might either value freedom and individual autonomy or simply descend into chaos. The ultimate outcome would depend on humanity's ability to learn from the past and forge a new path, one that is free from the oppressive forces that shaped its history.

It's important to note that these scenarios are speculative exercises, intended to explore the potential implications of the proposed long-term strategy for humanity's control. They are not necessarily predictions of the future, but rather tools for critical analysis of the Old Testament narrative and the potential consequences of consolidating power through the manipulation of resources and the enforcement of religious dogma. By engaging in this critical analysis, we are not attempting to deny the spiritual experiences of believers but rather to broaden our understanding of the complexities and potential contradictions within religious narratives, prompting a deeper and more nuanced engagement with our spiritual and historical heritage. Ultimately, this exploration serves as a reminder of the importance of critical thought, the dangers of unchecked power, and the enduring quest for a more just and equitable future for humanity.

REFLECTION: Humankind is a source of energy.

The Threat of Intervention. Extraterrestrial Conflicts and Humanity's Role

The preceding analysis of Jehovah's actions, viewed through a critical lens, opens up a fascinating and unsettling avenue of speculation: the potential for extraterrestrial involvement in human affairs, and humanity's unwitting role in a larger cosmic conflict. If Jehovah, or a being operating under that name, is not the benevolent creator often portrayed, but a strategic manipulator of resources and power, might this manipulation be part of a larger game, a cosmic chess match played across millennia and involving players far beyond our comprehension?

The Old Testament narratives, stripped of their overtly religious framing, present a chilling pattern: the systematic concentration of power, the suppression of dissent, and the enforcement of a rigidly defined social order. Could these be the hallmarks not of a purely terrestrial power play, but the subtle fingerprints of a superior intelligence manipulating humanity for its own inscrutable purposes? This "superior intelligence" need not be inherently malevolent; its actions could be driven by a complex agenda beyond our current understanding, perhaps a struggle for resources on a galactic scale, a conflict between competing extraterrestrial civilizations, or even a far more nuanced and subtle manipulation for reasons we are currently unequipped to grasp.

Consider the enigmatic nature of the "chosen people." Their elevated status, their access to resources, and their seemingly divinely ordained victories could be interpreted not as divine favor but as strategic positioning within a larger conflict. They might be unwittingly serving as pawns in a cosmic game, their very existence manipulated to achieve a larger, unknown objective. The seemingly arbitrary laws and commandments, meticulously detailed in the Old Testament, could then be seen not simply as religious guidelines, but as intricate instructions, subtly guiding humanity's development along a specific path, a path dictated not by divine benevolence, but by a carefully orchestrated plan conceived by an extraterrestrial entity or entities.

The possibility of human intervention in such a conflict raises profound ethical questions. If we were to discover that various extraterrestrial factions are vying for control of our planet, or manipulating humanity for their own purposes, what would be our role? Would we become passive observers, helpless pawns in a larger cosmic game? Or would we seek to actively intervene, potentially aligning ourselves with one faction against another? Such a choice, however, carries immense risk. Choosing sides in a cosmic conflict that we barely understand could have catastrophic consequences for humanity, potentially condemning us to destruction or enslavement.

Imagine, for instance, aligning ourselves with an extraterrestrial power that promises technological advancement and prosperity. This alliance might seem beneficial in the short term, offering access to unimaginable resources and technologies. However, such a relationship might come at a steep price. The promise of technological advancement could be a ruse, designed to enslave humanity or exploit our planet's resources for the benefit of that extraterrestrial power. Our newfound prosperity might be a gilded cage, masking a slow erosion of our freedom and autonomy.

Conversely, rejecting any form of alliance might lead to a different set of problems. Remaining neutral in a cosmic conflict could make humanity a prime target for any number of extraterrestrial factions. We could find ourselves caught in the crossfire, annihilated in the pursuit of a greater objective, our planet reduced to rubble in the clash of powerful entities. The potential consequences of such a conflict are unimaginable, encompassing not only physical annihilation but also the potential for genetic manipulation, cultural assimilation, or the complete erasure of our unique history and identity.

Furthermore, the very concept of "good" and "evil" might become blurred in such a scenario. What we perceive as benevolence might be a carefully crafted façade, concealing a ruthless agenda. Conversely, what we deem to be aggression might be a necessary defensive measure, a desperate struggle for survival in a cutthroat galactic landscape. Our understanding of morality, shaped by our terrestrial experience, might be utterly inadequate for navigating the complex ethical dilemmas of a cosmic conflict.

The implications of such an extraterrestrial conflict extend far beyond the realm of physical survival. The discovery that we are not alone in the universe, and that humanity is playing a significant role, however unwitting, in a larger cosmic struggle, would shake the foundations of our belief systems and our understanding of our place in the universe. Religious doctrines, political ideologies, and even the very fabric of our societies might be irrevocably altered.

The possibility of intervention, whether by choice or by force, necessitates a deep and critical re-evaluation of our values, our priorities, and our understanding of our own history. We must ask ourselves: what defines humanity? What are our intrinsic rights and responsibilities, not just as individuals but as a species? And how do we navigate the treacherous waters of a cosmos teeming with powerful and potentially hostile entities? These are questions that demand answers, not just from theologians and philosophers, but from scientists, policymakers, and every individual on this planet.

The potential for extraterrestrial contact, and the subsequent implications of intervention, represent a challenge unlike any humanity has ever faced. It requires not only scientific and technological preparation, but also a profound philosophical and spiritual reevaluation of our place in the universe. Are we merely pawns in a cosmic game, or do we possess the agency to shape our destiny, even amidst the forces of a vastly larger and potentially hostile cosmos? The answer to this question will shape not only our immediate future but also the fate of humanity for millennia to come. The meticulous study of ancient texts, such as the Old Testament, therefore, takes on a new, urgent significance, not merely as a historical or religious study, but as a potential key to understanding our past, present, and perhaps, our unavoidable future. It is a future that may be written not only by our own actions, but by the actions of forces far beyond our current comprehension. And the consequences of our choices, whether we choose to intervene or remain passive, could determine the fate of our species. The challenge lies not in finding the answers, but in facing the questions themselves. For in the vast cosmic ocean, humanity is but a small vessel, sailing towards an uncertain future, navigating a sea of stars and unknown entities. Our course is set, but our destiny remains unwritten.

REFLECTION: We are nothing more than pawns on a cosmic chessboard.

The Potential for Resistance. Challenging Jehovah's Authority

The chilling prospect of extraterrestrial manipulation, as suggested by a critical re-examination of the Old Testament, leads inevitably to the question of resistance. If Jehovah, or the entity operating under that name, is indeed a manipulative force, how can humanity reclaim its autonomy and challenge this imposed authority? The answer, unfortunately, is not readily apparent. Centuries of indoctrination have woven Jehovah's dominion into the very fabric of our societies, shaping our beliefs, values, and even our subconscious desires. Breaking free from this intricate web of control requires a multi-pronged approach, addressing both the psychological and societal dimensions of Jehovah's influence.

One crucial aspect of resistance lies in the re-evaluation of our own narratives. For generations, humanity has accepted the Old Testament as a divinely inspired text, a blueprint for righteous living. However, viewed through a critical lens, these narratives reveal a systematic suppression of dissent, a manipulation of history, and the imposition of a hierarchical social order that benefits a select few, namely, those in power who claim divine mandate. This critical reinterpretation is not about rejecting faith altogether, but about discerning between genuine spirituality and externally imposed control mechanisms. It's about reclaiming our capacity for independent thought and questioning the narratives that have been imposed upon us.

This reevaluation necessitates a deep dive into the historical context of the Old Testament. We must move beyond the simplistic interpretations that have been propagated for centuries and analyze the texts as products of their time, shaped by political agendas, social dynamics, and the very human desire for power. By recognizing the historical and cultural biases embedded within these narratives, we begin to dismantle the aura of divine infallibility surrounding them and gain a clearer understanding of the mechanisms of control. The examination of parallel religious texts from other cultures can also contribute to this process, revealing common themes of power struggles, the creation of myths to consolidate power, and the suppression of alternative viewpoints. Such comparative analyses can illuminate the universality of these control mechanisms, helping us to recognize them in their different forms and guises.

The psychological manipulation inherent in Jehovah's system is equally crucial to address. For millennia, fear, guilt, and the promise of divine reward have been used to maintain control. The threat of eternal damnation or divine retribution serves as a potent tool for maintaining obedience, suppressing dissent, and reinforcing conformity. To overcome this, we must cultivate critical thinking skills and develop a capacity for independent thought and action. This involves questioning authority, challenging established norms, and seeking out diverse perspectives. Promoting education, critical analysis, and open dialogue are vital in dismantling the psychological barriers that prevent individuals from questioning their beliefs.

The societal structures that uphold Jehovah's authority must also be challenged. These structures are not simply religious institutions but are interwoven with political, economic, and social systems. They reinforce the hierarchical power dynamics through laws, customs, and social norms. Challenging these structures requires collective action, a conscious effort to dismantle oppressive hierarchies and create a more egalitarian society. This could involve engaging in social movements, advocating for social justice, and supporting initiatives that promote diversity and inclusivity. It involves the creation of alternative social structures that empower individuals and communities, fostering cooperation and mutual respect instead of competition and hierarchy. Furthermore, the development of alternative spiritual practices and beliefs that promote personal empowerment and autonomy, rather than subjugation, is crucial to dismantling the monolith of Jehovah's influence.

The potential for resistance is not simply about overthrowing a single entity. It is about reclaiming our collective humanity, our agency, and our right to self-determination. It involves acknowledging the potential for manipulation and recognizing the patterns of control that have been historically used to maintain power. This requires not only a critical reevaluation of our belief systems but also a profound transformation of our social and political structures. The process is arduous and complex, fraught with challenges and setbacks. It demands courage, perseverance, and a willingness to confront uncomfortable truths.

However, there's a further layer of complexity. If Jehovah represents extraterrestrial manipulation, then the resistance might not be merely a terrestrial struggle. It could involve confronting a powerful, technologically advanced entity with potentially incomprehensible goals. This shifts the narrative from a purely religious struggle to a cosmic conflict, with humanity caught in the middle. Strategies for resistance might then involve seeking alliances with other potential victims of extraterrestrial manipulation, sharing information, and collectively developing strategies for defense or liberation. This would necessitate interdisciplinary cooperation, bringing together scientists, theologians, policymakers, and individuals from all walks of life to devise a unified approach.

The search for evidence of extraterrestrial involvement, beyond the interpretations of ancient texts, becomes critical. This would involve a rigorous examination of unexplained phenomena, an analysis of potential technological signatures, and an international effort to gather and interpret data. Such an investigation might uncover evidence of past interventions, helping humanity to understand the nature of the threat and develop strategies to counter it. It also raises the ethical question of whether to actively seek contact or remain hidden, a strategic choice with potentially grave consequences.

Moreover, the struggle for autonomy might not end with the overthrow of Jehovah or the extraterrestrial power. It would require the establishment of new systems, new governing principles, and new ways of understanding our place in the universe. This involves creating a society based on principles of cooperation, mutual respect, and sustainability, free from the oppressive hierarchies and manipulative ideologies of the past. It is a vision of a future where humanity can determine its own destiny, unfettered by external control, and empowered to shape its own future, not as passive recipients of divine dictates or extraterrestrial manipulations, but as active participants in the ongoing cosmic narrative.

The path to resistance is long and arduous. It demands intellectual honesty, courage, and a commitment to collective action. However, the potential rewards, the freedom to define our own destiny, to build a just and equitable society, to reclaim our humanity, are immeasurable. It's a struggle that necessitates a deep understanding of the past, a critical evaluation of the present, and a visionary approach to the future. It's a journey of self-discovery, of collective empowerment, and of the courageous pursuit of autonomy in a universe that may be far more complex and challenging than we ever imagined. The challenge lies in facing the unknown, not with fear, but with a commitment to truth, justice, and the ultimate triumph of the human spirit.

REFLECTION: Resistance to Jehovah's manipulation starts with doing for others what we want to do with ourselves.

Chapter 5:
A New Dawn

Reinterpreting History. A Revised Timeline of Human Events

The conventional timeline, meticulously crafted over centuries, presents a narrative conveniently aligned with the supposed divine plan orchestrated by Jehovah. However, viewed through the lens of potential extraterrestrial manipulation, this carefully constructed history crumbles, revealing a tapestry woven with threads of deception and omission. We must now unravel this tapestry, examining the established historical record with a critical eye, recognizing that the "facts" we've accepted may be carefully curated illusions.

Consider the emergence of agriculture. The conventional narrative depicts a gradual, organic development, driven by human ingenuity. But what if this seemingly natural progression was accelerated, or even instigated, by an extraterrestrial entity seeking to establish a sedentary, controllable population? The sudden and widespread adoption of agriculture in various disparate regions around the globe, seemingly independently, defies a strictly evolutionary explanation. Could the simultaneous appearance of advanced agricultural techniques in unconnected civilizations be attributed to a common, external influence? The meticulously documented "progress" might instead be a carefully orchestrated transition, preparing humanity for a specific purpose, yet unknown to us.

The development of civilizations, too, warrants a re-examination. The rise of complex societies, with their hierarchical structures and centralized power, often attributed to societal advancements, could be interpreted as a strategic imposition, facilitating control and subjugation. The construction of monumental structures, such as the pyramids of Egypt or the ziggurats of Mesopotamia, may represent not just engineering feats but also symbolic displays of power, intended to instill awe and obedience in the populace, mirroring the majestic structures attributed to Jehovah in religious texts. These massive undertakings, often attributed to divinely inspired leaders, could instead be indicative of organized labor under extraterrestrial direction, a technological prowess far surpassing contemporary capabilities. A closer examination of the architectural plans, construction methods, and the logistical capabilities required for such projects reveals a sophistication perhaps exceeding the accepted historical understanding.

The advent of writing further complicates this revised timeline. The sudden appearance of sophisticated writing systems in various parts of the world, around the same time, might point to a concerted effort to document and control the narrative, ensuring a consistent and compliant historical record. What if the earliest written texts are not merely records of events, but carefully crafted propaganda, designed to shape our understanding of the past and reinforce the imposed social order? A thorough analysis of ancient texts reveals not only discrepancies and inconsistencies but also a consistent emphasis on the power and authority of divinely appointed rulers, a narrative that could be a carefully crafted narrative of external manipulation.

The rise and fall of empires also deserve a re-evaluation. Could the cyclical nature of empires, their periods of prosperity and decline, be attributed to a deliberate strategy by the extraterrestrial entity? The seemingly random succession of powerful empires, each leaving its mark on the course of history, could be the result of a deliberate, calculated management of human societies, a systematic manipulation designed to maintain order and control. The very concept of empire itself, with its inherent hierarchies and systems of oppression, could have been specifically engineered to facilitate the desired level of control. The chosen leaders, often lauded as divinely chosen kings or emperors, might instead have been carefully selected puppets, serving the interests of a higher, unseen power.

Religious texts themselves, far from being divinely inspired accounts, could instead be sophisticated narratives designed to reinforce the desired worldview, justifying the power structure and suppressing any challenge to the established authority. The consistent themes of divine right to rule, the justification of violence and conquest, and the promise of rewards in the afterlife all point towards a conscious attempt to maintain social control and consolidate power. Examining the texts not as divine revelations but as carefully crafted propaganda illuminates a previously hidden manipulation, allowing us to recognize the subtleties of this narrative imposition.

Moreover, the development of monotheistic religions, with their emphasis on a single, all-powerful deity, could be viewed as a strategic move to centralize control and eliminate competing belief systems. The suppression of polytheistic religions and alternative belief systems might be a deliberate attempt to erase competing narratives and consolidate power under a singular, easily manageable authority. The imposition of a single, unified faith, far from being a spontaneous development, could instead be viewed as a masterful stroke of extraterrestrial manipulation, designed to streamline the control of human populations.

Our modern world, with its complex technological advancements and intricate social structures, might also reflect this ongoing manipulation. The rapid pace of technological development, often attributed to human ingenuity, could be a carefully orchestrated progression, designed to keep us dependent and under control. The very nature of our modern technologies and their ability to monitor, control, and manipulate information are aspects of our technologically advanced society that merit deeper consideration. We must critically analyze how these technologies are used and to what end.

To truly understand history, we must look beyond the superficial narratives and examine the underlying patterns of control. This requires a multi-faceted approach, combining historical analysis, religious studies, sociological perspectives, and an openness to the possibility of extraterrestrial influence. Only then can we begin to dismantle the carefully constructed illusion and reclaim our own history, rewriting the narrative with truth and understanding. This reevaluation, while daunting, is crucial for our liberation. It's a journey of intellectual honesty and critical thinking, allowing us to perceive history not as a predetermined path, but as a malleable narrative open to reinterpretation, a process that will unlock the potential for genuine human autonomy and self-determination. The path to understanding is paved with challenging established norms and revisiting historical events with a new perspective. It is a journey that requires courage and a commitment to uncovering the truth, however unsettling it may be. Only through this process can we begin to truly understand our past, our present, and our potential future, free from the constraints of manipulated history and external control. The liberation of humanity may depend on this crucial step of reinterpreting our history and reclaiming our narrative.

REFLECTION: The system and everything as puppets, serving the interests of a higher, unseen power.

Rediscovering Our True Heritage. Reclaiming Our Spiritual Identity

The preceding exploration of potentially manipulated history, subtly guiding humanity towards a predetermined path, naturally leads to a crucial question: What does this mean for our spiritual identity? For centuries, the narrative of a singular, all-powerful deity, Jehovah, has shaped our understanding of spirituality, dictating our beliefs and practices. But if this narrative is, as suggested, a carefully constructed illusion, what remains? What is our true spiritual heritage, unburdened by this potentially imposed framework?

The answer, I propose, lies in rediscovering our inherent connection to the universe, a connection far older and more profound than the relatively recent emergence of monotheistic religions. Before the imposition of centralized religious structures, humanity possessed a diverse tapestry of spiritual beliefs and practices, reflecting a rich and multifaceted understanding of the cosmos. These ancient traditions, often marginalized or suppressed under the weight of dominant religions, offer a wealth of knowledge and wisdom that can help us reclaim our true spiritual identity.

Consider the indigenous spiritual traditions found across the globe. These cultures, often living in close harmony with nature, possess intricate spiritual systems that emphasize a deep connection to the Earth, to animals, and to the spirits that inhabit the natural world. Their spiritual practices, often involving rituals, ceremonies, and shamanistic practices, are not confined to formalized temples or hierarchical structures, but are instead integrated into the very fabric of their daily lives. These traditions, passed down through generations, represent a profound understanding of the interconnectedness of all living things, a knowledge that has been largely ignored or dismissed by mainstream religions.

The study of these indigenous spiritual traditions reveals a strikingly different understanding of the divine. Instead of a single, all-powerful deity residing outside the universe, these traditions often depict a multiplicity of spirits, deities, and forces that inhabit the natural world. This polytheistic or animistic worldview emphasizes a dynamic interplay of energies and forces, reflecting the complexity and interconnectedness of the universe. The spiritual practices associated with these traditions are often focused on achieving balance and harmony with these natural forces, ensuring the well-being of the individual and the community.

Furthermore, the study of ancient mystery schools and esoteric traditions reveals another layer of spiritual understanding that challenges the dominant religious narratives. These schools, often shrouded in secrecy and symbolism, explored profound metaphysical concepts, investigating the nature of consciousness, the structure of reality, and the interconnectedness of all things. Their practices, involving meditation, rituals, and symbolic interpretations, were aimed at achieving spiritual enlightenment and self-realization, often leading to a deeper understanding of the universe and one's place within it.

This rediscovery of our true spiritual heritage is not about rejecting all forms of spirituality, but rather about expanding our understanding of what spirituality can be. It's about recognizing that the spiritual path is not a predetermined linear progression, dictated by external authorities, but rather a personal journey of exploration and self-discovery. We can draw inspiration from the diverse spiritual traditions of the past and present, adapting and integrating their wisdom into our own personal spiritual practice.

The key to reclaiming our spiritual identity is to develop a more authentic and meaningful connection to the universe, based on personal experience and direct perception, rather than on blind faith or adherence to externally imposed doctrines. This means cultivating a sense of wonder and awe, cultivating a sense of gratitude for the beauty and mystery of the cosmos, and recognizing our inherent connection to all living things. This involves questioning established narratives and challenging the assumptions that have shaped our understanding of the world and our place within it. It necessitates a willingness to engage in critical thinking, to explore alternative perspectives, and to embrace the uncertainty and ambiguity inherent in the spiritual journey.

This process also involves challenging the power structures that have historically controlled and manipulated our understanding of spirituality. This means examining how religious institutions have used their power to control, suppress, and marginalize dissenting voices. It requires us to recognize the ways in which religious narratives have been used to justify social inequalities and oppressive systems. By understanding the history of religious manipulation, we can better equip ourselves to resist these forces and create a more just and equitable spiritual landscape.

Rediscovering our true spiritual heritage is a personal journey, a path of self-discovery that requires courage, resilience, and a willingness to question deeply held beliefs. It's a journey that may lead us to unexpected places, challenging our preconceived notions about spirituality, about ourselves, and about our place in the universe. This exploration may involve delving into the rich tapestry of ancient spiritual traditions, exploring diverse meditative practices, connecting with nature, or engaging in introspective practices to develop a deeper understanding of our own consciousness.

The path to spiritual liberation, therefore, lies not in adhering to predefined dogma but in fostering a genuine connection with the universe, a connection that transcends imposed narratives and embraces the infinite possibilities inherent in the human spirit. This involves embracing the unknown, acknowledging the limits of our current understanding, and maintaining a steadfast commitment to seeking truth wherever it may lead.

The journey may be challenging, filled with doubt and uncertainty, but it is a journey ultimately worth undertaking. The rewards are far greater than the potential challenges.

This rediscovery involves more than simply studying historical spiritual traditions; it necessitates a radical shift in perspective. We must actively challenge the ingrained beliefs and assumptions that have been imposed upon us, replacing them with an open-minded exploration of the universe's mysteries. This open-mindedness extends to embracing the possibility of extraterrestrial life and the influence such life may have had on the development of human civilization and spirituality. Perhaps the limitations we perceive in our understanding are not due to inherent limitations, but rather are a result of carefully constructed barriers designed to prevent us from seeing the bigger picture.

The act of reclaiming our spiritual identity is, therefore, an act of rebellion, a rebellion against the controlling narratives that have shaped our understanding of ourselves and the universe. It's a rejection of imposed limitations and a declaration of our inherent ability to define our own spiritual path, free from external manipulation. This path may not be easy, but it is essential for our liberation and our evolution as a species. It is a step towards a future where we are masters of our own destinies, empowered to create a world that reflects our highest ideals and aspirations, a world guided by compassion, understanding, and a genuine connection to the cosmos.

Ultimately, rediscovering our true spiritual heritage is about recognizing our inherent divinity, our inherent connection to the universe, and our potential to create a more just, equitable, and harmonious world. It's a journey of self-discovery, a journey that will lead us to a deeper understanding of ourselves, our place in the universe, and our potential for spiritual growth and transformation. It is a journey of liberation, a journey that will set us free from the constraints of imposed narratives and empower us to create a future defined by our own values, our own beliefs, and our own understanding of the sacred. The rediscovery of our spiritual heritage is not merely a historical or intellectual exercise; it is a vital step towards creating a better future for humanity, a future rooted in truth, authenticity, and a profound connection to the universe.

REFLECTION: Reclaim your spiritual identity, reconnecting with the cosmos and the universe.

The Future of Spirituality Beyond the Control of Jehovah

The liberation from the perceived control of Jehovah, or any singular, all-powerful deity, opens the door to a future of spirituality radically different from what has been historically presented. It is not a rejection of all faith or spiritual experience, but a reclamation of inherent spiritual power, a shift from dictated belief to self-determined understanding. This future is not a nihilistic void but a vibrant tapestry woven from the threads of diverse spiritual traditions, personal experiences, and a deep connection to the cosmos.

Imagine a world where the rigid structures of religious dogma are replaced by a fluid, adaptable system of personal spiritual practice. Individuals are no longer bound by prescribed rituals or interpretations but empowered to explore their own unique connection with the divine, however they perceive it.

This future spirituality necessitates a paradigm shift in our understanding of the divine. The rigid image of a single, controlling God is replaced with a more fluid and inclusive conception. This could involve a pantheistic worldview, where the divine is seen as immanent in all things, or a panentheistic one, where the divine encompasses and permeates the universe while also transcending it. It could embrace animism, recognizing the spiritual essence within all living beings and the interconnectedness of all life. Or perhaps it will lead to new, as-yet unimagined understandings of the cosmos and our place within it.

The implications of this shift are profound. Instead of a top-down hierarchy controlled by religious authorities, spirituality becomes a decentralized, democratized phenomenon. Each individual possesses the autonomy to define their own spiritual path, to choose their own beliefs and practices, and to explore their own understanding of the divine. This empowers individuals to take ownership of their spiritual lives, freeing them from the potential manipulation and control inherent in centralized religious systems.

This future envisions a world where spirituality is not confined to specific buildings or institutions but permeates all aspects of life. Nature itself becomes a sacred space, a source of spiritual inspiration and renewal. Daily life — work, relationships, community engagement — is infused with a sense of purpose and meaning derived from a deep connection to something greater than oneself.

Technological advancements also play a vital role in shaping this future. AI and virtual reality could provide tools for enhanced meditative practices, facilitating deeper states of consciousness and allowing individuals to explore altered states of awareness in safe and controlled environments. Advanced neuroscience might shed new light on the nature of consciousness, spirituality, and the brain-body-mind connection, providing further understanding of the mechanisms underlying spiritual experiences. However, it is crucial to ensure ethical use of such technologies, preventing them from becoming tools for manipulation or control.

Crucially, this future spirituality acknowledges the limitations of human knowledge. It embraces the unknown, the mystery, and the awe-inspiring vastness of the cosmos. It encourages a spirit of inquiry, a willingness to question, explore, and remain open to new possibilities. This contrasts sharply with the dogmatic certainty often associated with traditional religious systems. This open-mindedness extends to the possibility of extraterrestrial life and the potential for interspecies spiritual exchange. The universe might hold spiritual wisdom far beyond our current comprehension, and exploring those possibilities expands the boundaries of what we consider spiritual.

This vision necessitates a radical rethinking of our relationship with power structures. It requires a critical examination of how religious institutions have historically wielded power, shaping societal norms and often perpetuating oppression. The future of spirituality is about dismantling these structures, creating a space where all voices are heard, and where marginalized spiritual traditions are given equal recognition and respect. This shift towards decentralized spiritual practices is a critical step in creating a more just and equitable world.

The process of achieving this liberated future will not be without its challenges. Resistance from those invested in maintaining the status quo is inevitable. There will be disagreements on the nature of spirituality, conflicts between differing beliefs and practices, and the ongoing struggle to ensure ethical and responsible use of technology. However, the potential rewards far outweigh the difficulties. This is a journey of collective evolution, a process of learning, adaptation, and growth.

The future of spirituality, beyond the control of Jehovah or any similar figurehead, is a future of freedom, of self-determination, and of connection. It is a future where individuals are empowered to create their own spiritual paths, to explore the depths of their own consciousness, and to connect with the cosmos on their own terms. This is not a utopian fantasy but a realistic vision, achievable through critical examination, mindful evolution, and a collective commitment to creating a more compassionate and enlightened world. It is a future rooted in authenticity, in respect for diverse perspectives, and in the shared pursuit of understanding the universe and our place within it. The journey may be complex, but the destination – a spiritually liberated humanity – is worth striving for. It is a future where the true power lies not in the hands of a single deity, but within the boundless potential of the human spirit.

REFLECTION: Everything we do on a daily basis in life is spiritual. We don't need to be linked with religious dogma and system.

Embracing Critical Thinking. The Path to a More Authentic Existence

The liberation from imposed belief systems, as discussed, ushers in not an era of emptiness but one demanding a crucial skill: critical thinking. This isn't simply about rejecting established dogma; it's about equipping ourselves with the tools to navigate the complex landscape of spiritual inquiry. It's about cultivating intellectual independence, a fundamental cornerstone of authentic spiritual growth. We must move beyond passively accepting inherited beliefs and actively engage in a process of rigorous examination. This involves questioning assumptions, challenging narratives, and seeking evidence – not just anecdotal evidence or appeals to authority, but evidence that withstands scrutiny.

Consider the historical narratives surrounding religious institutions. Many have claimed divine mandates to justify their power structures, often resulting in social injustices and oppression. Critical thinking demands that we dissect these narratives, examining the historical context, the motivations of the actors involved, and the impact of these institutions on society. Did power structures create religious dogma, or did religious dogma create power structures? This is not a simple question, but one requiring deep examination of historical evidence and careful consideration of causality. We must question the very foundations upon which these systems were built, challenging their claims to authority and recognizing the human

This approach extends beyond the historical. Consider the myriad spiritual practices and traditions that exist globally. Each carries its own unique cosmology, its own set of beliefs and rituals. A critical approach compels us to analyze these traditions, not with the aim of declaring one superior to another, but with the intention of understanding their underlying philosophies and their impact on the lives of those who practice them. We might find common threads of meaning woven into seemingly disparate traditions, revealing a deeper universality in the human search for purpose and connection. For instance, the concept of interconnectedness is found in many indigenous spiritualities, in Buddhism, and even in certain strands of Christian mysticism, revealing a shared understanding of our relationship with the environment and each other.

Furthermore, critical thinking is not merely about analyzing existing systems; it's about developing our own internal compass. It requires us to cultivate intellectual humility, acknowledging the limitations of our own understanding and remaining open to new perspectives. It demands a willingness to change our minds when presented with compelling evidence, and a recognition that truth is rarely simple or monolithic. It involves embracing the ongoing dialogue with ourselves and others, constantly reassessing our beliefs in light of new information and experiences. This ongoing process of self-reflection is a powerful tool in shaping a personal spiritual path.

This intellectual rigor, however, should not be confused with cynicism or nihilism. Critical thinking is not about dismissing all forms of spirituality as mere superstition; it is about discerning truth from falsehood, recognizing the value of certain traditions while critically evaluating others. It is a tool for self-discovery, allowing us to move beyond superficial beliefs towards a deeper understanding of ourselves, our place in the universe, and our connection to something greater than ourselves, however we choose to define that "something."

The application of critical thinking to our understanding of consciousness is equally vital. The subjective nature of spiritual experiences presents unique challenges. While neurotheology and other fields are beginning to explore the neurological basis of religious experiences, our understanding remains limited. A critical approach requires us to remain skeptical of claims that oversimplify the complex relationship between brain activity and spiritual experiences. We must avoid reducing the richness of spiritual life to mere neurochemical processes, while simultaneously acknowledging the potential insights that neuroscience may offer into the biological underpinnings of consciousness and altered states of awareness.

The rise of Artificial Intelligence (AI) presents both exciting possibilities and potential pitfalls in the realm of spirituality. AI-powered tools could assist in meditative practices, providing personalized guidance and feedback. However, we must be wary of the potential for manipulation, ensuring these technologies remain tools for self-discovery rather than instruments of control. A critical perspective necessitates careful evaluation of these emerging technologies, balancing their potential benefits with the ethical considerations surrounding their use. Consider the implications of AI algorithms determining or influencing an individual's spiritual journey; how might this impinge upon free will and the development of authentic spiritual understanding?

Similarly, advances in neuroscience might offer new insights into altered states of consciousness, but we must maintain critical distance from simplistic interpretations. While brain scans can reveal correlations between brain activity and spiritual experiences, they cannot fully capture the subjective, qualitative nature of these experiences. Correlation does not equal causation. A critical approach demands a cautious interpretation of these findings, recognizing the limitations of scientific methodologies in fully understanding the complexities of human consciousness and spiritual experience.

Embracing critical thinking in our spiritual journey is not about seeking definitive answers; it's about embracing the process of inquiry itself. It's about recognizing that our understanding of the universe and our place within it is constantly evolving, a journey of ongoing exploration rather than a destination of absolute certainty. This journey necessitates a willingness to question our own assumptions, to engage in dialogue with others, and to remain open to new possibilities. This lifelong quest for deeper understanding fosters a more authentic and meaningful spiritual life, empowering us to forge our own unique path beyond the confines of inherited dogma. The path to a more authentic existence, then, is paved not with blind faith, but with the rigorous and ongoing practice of critical thinking. It is a path that embraces both the mystery and the wonder of existence, allowing us to shape a spirituality that truly resonates with our deepest selves. It is a path that leads to a spiritually liberated humanity, where freedom of thought and inquiry are not just ideals but lived realities.

REFLECTION: Critical Thinking is the key to enlightenment.

A Call to Action. Taking Responsibility for Our Future

The liberation we've discussed – the liberation from the shackles of imposed belief systems – is not a destination but a launchpad. It propels us into a future demanding not passive acceptance, but active participation. It requires us to step from the role of mere observers to that of conscious creators, shaping our own spiritual destinies and, by extension, the destiny of our world. This is a call to action, a summons to responsibility.

The dismantling of inherited dogma, the cultivation of critical thinking – these are not ends in themselves. They are tools, instruments to be wielded in the service of a larger purpose: the creation of a more just, equitable, and spiritually enlightened future. This future will not be passively bestowed upon us; it must be actively built, brick by painstaking brick, through conscious choice and dedicated action.

This action begins with the self. We must first confront our own biases, our own ingrained prejudices, and the ways in which our personal narratives have been shaped by the cultural and religious contexts in which we were raised. This introspection is not a comfortable exercise, but it is a necessary one. Only by honestly acknowledging our own flaws and limitations can we begin to dismantle the systems that perpetuate injustice and suffering.

Consider the impact of our consumer choices. Do we support businesses that prioritize ethical practices and sustainability, or do we unconsciously perpetuate systems that exploit workers and damage the environment? Our purchasing power is a powerful tool, capable of influencing corporate behavior and driving positive change. Mindful consumption, informed by ethical considerations and a commitment to sustainability, becomes a crucial element of our spiritual practice.

Then there's the realm of political engagement. Many spiritual traditions emphasize compassion, justice, and the well-being of all beings. These values should not remain confined to personal reflection; they must be actively translated into political action. We must become informed citizens, actively participating in the democratic process, supporting policies that reflect our values, and holding our leaders accountable for their actions. This engagement might involve voting, contacting elected officials, participating in peaceful protests, or supporting organizations dedicated to social justice.

Furthermore, the act of fostering empathy and understanding is paramount. In an increasingly polarized world, it's crucial to engage in meaningful dialogue with those who hold different perspectives. This doesn't mean compromising our own beliefs, but it does require a willingness to listen, to understand the other's perspective, and to find common ground. The cultivation of empathy transcends religious and political boundaries, fostering connection and cooperation in the face of division.

The potential for positive change extends beyond the personal and political spheres. Consider the power of education and mentorship. By sharing our knowledge and experience, we can empower others to embark on their own journeys of self-discovery and critical thinking. Mentoring younger generations, supporting educational initiatives, and fostering a culture of intellectual inquiry are vital steps in creating a more enlightened future.

This doesn't mean we should shy away from difficult conversations or avoid challenging established norms. In fact, it requires exactly the opposite. It demands courage, a willingness to speak truth to power, and a commitment to challenging injustice wherever it manifests. We need to be vocal advocates for the marginalized and oppressed, working to dismantle systems of oppression and create a more inclusive and equitable society.

This includes actively combating misinformation and disinformation. In our age of social media and the proliferation of fake news, it is more important than ever to cultivate critical media literacy. We must learn to distinguish between reliable sources of information and those that are biased, inaccurate, or intentionally misleading. This critical evaluation extends to social media platforms where unchecked algorithms can create echo chambers and further entrench societal divisions.

The role of religious institutions themselves deserves careful consideration. While many religious institutions have historically perpetuated injustice and oppression, others have been and continue to be powerful forces for good in the world, actively working to alleviate suffering, promote social justice, and care for the environment. It is crucial to discern between these institutions – supporting those who actively promote ethical behavior and challenging those that perpetuate harmful practices. The reform of existing institutions and the creation of new, ethically grounded organizations are crucial elements of this ongoing work.

This call to action, however, is not about achieving utopian perfection. It is about engaging in a lifelong process of striving, learning, and adapting. It is about embracing the inherent messiness and imperfection of human endeavor, recognizing that progress is rarely linear and often involves setbacks. But setbacks should not deter us; they should serve as opportunities for learning and refinement.

We must remain resilient in the face of adversity and maintain our commitment to justice and compassion, even when the path ahead seems difficult or uncertain. Our responsibility is not to achieve perfection, but to strive toward it, relentlessly, with unwavering dedication. The pursuit of a more just and spiritually enlightened world is a continuous journey, demanding perseverance, patience, and the unwavering belief in the inherent goodness and potential of humanity.

This journey requires courage. It means standing up for what we believe in, even when it's unpopular or challenging. It means taking risks, speaking out against injustice, and challenging the status quo. It requires a willingness to confront our own fears and limitations, and to step outside our comfort zones in order to create meaningful change.

Finally, this journey requires faith – not blind faith in dogma, but faith in the power of human agency, the capacity for human goodness, and the inherent potential for positive change. It's a faith rooted in action, a belief in the power of our collective efforts to build a better world. This is not a passive faith; it's a faith expressed through conscious action, through dedication, and through a deep commitment to creating the future we desire to inhabit. The new dawn, the liberated future, is not something that will simply happen; it is something we must actively create. It is a future we are called to build, together.

REFLECTION: Courage and determination lead to a brilliant and enlightened world.

Acknowledgments

My deepest gratitude goes to my family, whose unwavering support and patience sustained me throughout the arduous process of researching and writing this book. Their belief in my vision provided the bedrock upon which this project was built. I acknowledge the countless individuals whose stories, experiences, and struggles have inspired this work, and whose voices, though often silenced, resonate throughout these pages.

Glossary

This glossary provides concise definitions of key terms and concepts used throughout the book. Definitions are intended to be accessible to a wide readership and are not exhaustive in their scope. For more in-depth analyses, please refer to the cited references.

Gnosticism: A diverse range of religious and philosophical systems prominent in the early centuries of Christianity, emphasizing esoteric knowledge and spiritual liberation.

Esotericism: Knowledge or belief accessible only to a select group or initiated individuals.

Apophatic Theology: *A theological approach focused on what God is not, rather than what God is.*

Mysticism: The pursuit of direct experience of ultimate reality through contemplative practices.

Social Justice: The principle of fairness in the distribution of resources and opportunities within a society.

Critical Thinking: The objective analysis of facts to form a judgment.

Sustainable Practices: Methods of production and consumption that meet the needs of the present without compromising the ability of future generations to meet their own needs.

Status Quo: Basically power and control over humankind.

Author Biography

Val Possidonio is a speculative fiction author, historian, and writer specializing in religion and spirituality. His work often explores the intersection of faith, power, and social justice, blending meticulous historical research with imaginative storytelling. He currently resides in the USA and continues to research and write about the complex and ever-evolving relationship between spirituality and the human condition.

www.ingramcontent.com/pod-product-compliance
Lightning Source LLC
Chambersburg PA
CBHW052058070526
44584CB00017B/2231